12 SERMONS to YOUNG PEOPLE

Charles H. Spurgeon

BAKER BOOK HOUSE
Grand Rapids, Michigan

Contents

Paperback edition
issued 1976 by
Baker Book House

ISBN: 0-8010-8065-7

First Printing, February 1976
Second Printing, March 1977
Third Printing, September 1978

Formerly printed under
the title:
Twelve Sermons to Young Men

1   A Young Man's Vision

" Your young men shall see visions."—Acts ii. 17.

MANY visions have led to the most disastrous results.   When Napoleon had a vision of a universal monarchy over which he should preside, with the French eagle for his ensign, he drenched the lands in blood.   Many visions have been wretchedly delusive.   Men have dreamed of finding the fairy pleasure in the dark forest of sin.   Carnal joys have danced before their eyes as temptingly as the *mirage* in the desert, and they have pursued the phantom forms to their misery in this world, and to their eternal ruin in the next.   Mistaking license for liberty, and madness for mirth, they have dreamed themselves into hell. Many dreams have been enervating—sucking the life-blood out of men as vampires do.   Men have passed from stern reality into dream-land, and while seemingly awakened, have continued like somnambulists to do all things in their sleep.   Many pass all their days in one perpetual day-dream, speculating, building castles in the air, thinking of what they would do—if, and vowing how they would behave themselves— suppose.   With fine capacities they have drivelled away existence: as their theory of life was born of smoke, so the result of their lives has been a cloud.   The luxurious indolence of mere resolve, the useless tossings of regret—these have been all their sluggard life.

For all this, good and grand visions are not unknown—visions which came from the excellent glory ; visions which, when young or old men have seen them, have filled them with wisdom, and grace, and holiness; visions which have wrought with such effect upon their minds that they have been lifted up above the level of the sons of men, and made sons of God, co-workers with the Eternal.   Such visions are given to men whose eyes have been illumined by the Holy Spirit—visions which have come of that eye-salve which only the Holy Ghost can apply ; visions which are not bestowed on carnal men, nor unveiled to the impure in heart ; visions reserved for the men elect of God, who are sanctified by the Holy Ghost, and made meet to be partakers of the witness of God and the testimony of his Son.

All divine things, when they first come to men from the Lord, are as visions, because man is so little prepared to believe God's thoughts and ways, that he cannot think them to be real. They appear to us to be too great, too good to be real, and we look at them rather as things to be desired and wished for than as things that may be actually ours. It must be so while Jehovah's ways are higher than our ways, and his thoughts than our thoughts. It must be so, that even divine mercy should at first be a burden to the prophet who has its message to deliver, and that the eternal promise should be a vision to the seer who first receives it. We are so gross and carnal, even when most clarified and made fit to receive divine impressions, that God's spiritual messages and directions to us must usually at the first float dimly before the sense, and only in after thoughts become solid and clear. We must take care that we do not neglect heavenly monitions through fear of being considered visionary; we must not be staggered even by the dread of being styled fanatical, or out of our minds, for to stifle a thought from God is no mean sin.

How much of good in this world would have been lost if good men had quenched the first half-fashioned thoughts which have flitted before them! I mean, for instance, had Martin Luther taken the advice of his teacher when he said to him, " Go thy way, silly monk! Go to thy cell, and pray God, and if it be his will he will reform the abuses of this church, but what hast thou to do with it?" Supposing the agitated monk had administered an opiate to his soul, what then? Doubtless the gospel to Luther at the first was dim enough, and the idea of reform most vague and indistinct, but had he closed his heart to his vision, how long might not the Romish darkness have brooded over the multitudes of Europe? And George Fox, that most eminent of dreamers, who dreamed more and more vividly than any other man, where had been all the testimonies for a spiritual religion, where all the holy influences for benevolence, for peace, for anti-slavery, for I know not what besides, which have streamed upon this world through the agency of the Society of Friends, if the wild Quaker had been content to let his impressions come and go and be forgotten? These things, which nowadays are ordinary Christian doctrines, were considered in his day to be but the prattle of fanatics; even as the reforms which some of us shall live to see are denounced as revolutionary, or ridiculed as Utopian. O young men, if you have received a thought which dashes ahead of your times, hold to it and work at it till it comes to something. If you have dreamed a dream from the Lord, turn it over and over again till you are quite sure it is not steam from a heated brain, or smoke from hell, and when it is clear to your own heart that it is fire from off God's altar, then work and pray, and wait your time. Perhaps it may take fifty years to work that thought out, or what is worse, you may never live to see it realised, but what of that? *You* may have to leave that thought sown in the dust, but the thought will not die, but produce a harvest when you are with the angels. Do not, I pray you, because the thing happens to seem new, or too enthusiastic, or too far ahead, be snubbed into putting it into a corner, but take care of it, and nurture it; and if it be not of God, a little experience will disabuse you of it let us hope; but if it be of the Lord, you will grow in your attachment to it, and by-and-by God will find an opportunity for you to make it practical. The great Father of spirits does, in fact, say to you when he puts a great design into your keeping, as Pharaoh's daughter said to Jochebed, "Take this child away, and nurse it for me, and I will give thee thy wages;" and though the Moses that you nurse may not deliver Israel in your lifetime, yet shall you have your wages if you nurse the thought for God.

Many suggestions which come from God to men, are not so much visions to them as they are to the outside world. And need we wonder at this? Why, men of science and art have to endure the same ordeal. Stephenson declares that he will make a machine which will run without horse-power, at the rate of twelve miles an hour—and how the Tory benches of the House of Commons, loaded then as now with stupidity, roared at the man as a born fool! How was it proved to a demonstration that if the engine began to work, the wheels might revolve, but the engine never would move an inch! Or if it moved at a great speed, the passengers would not be able to breathe! Yet Stephenson lived to see his dream fulfilled, and we have lived to see it a much more wonderful power still. Now, if men of science can endure this, and if we members of the Baptist Mission recollect still the roars of laughter which were launched by Sydney Smith against " the inspired cobbler," when he talked about the conquest of India for the Lord Jesus Christ, we may well be prepared, when we obtain an inspiration from God, to put up with a world of scorn, and opposition, and contempt for a little time, and to say, " Never mind, there is a day coming that shall reverse the hasty judgment of this world; you sons of darkness, are not a fair jury to sit upon questions of light; you blind men who know not God, nor the glory of his power, are not qualified to mount the bench and sit in judgment upon thoughts which flash from the eternal mind. You may give your judgment, but the Lord shall reverse it, and time, which is always with truth, will ere long turn the laugh in another direction.

With this rather too long preface about dreaming, I will now confess that, after my own fashion, I, too, have seen a vision ; and though you should say of me in days to come, "Behold, this dreamer cometh," yet, as he that hath a dream is bidden to tell his dream, so tell I mine. My dream is this: I have seen in vision missionary spirit in England, now so given to slumber, marvellously quickened, awakened, and revived. I have seen—the wish was father to the sight—I have seen the ardour of our first missionary days return to us; I have seen young men eager for the mission field, and old men and fathers sitting in united council to correct mistakes, to devise new methods, or to strengthen the old ones, so that by any means the great chariot of Christ might roll onwards, and that his victories might be more rapid. I thought that I saw, from one end of England to the other, the Christian church stirred with a deep sense of her duty to the heathen ; Christian ministers full of pangs and sorrows on account of dying myriads; Christian men and women universally contributing liberally of their substance, while men fitted for the work pushed forward at the call of the great Lord of the harvest to toil in the great harvest-field. I have seen such a vision. By God's grace, we shall see it a fact ! Would to God that the captivity of our Zion might be turned, then should we be like them that dream; then should our mouth be filled with laughter and our tongue with singing, while the heathen would cry, "The Lord hath done great things for them."

First, this evening, I shall *try to justify my vision, and show that it is by no means unreasonable;* secondly, I shall, in a few words, *elaborate the vision, or give the details of it;* and then, in the third place, as time may suit us, shall endeavour to *promote its realisation.*

I. First, LET US JUSTIFY OUR VISION.

We have dreamed that the missionary spirit was suddenly revived among us, that missions were pushed on with greater ardour, and that God vouchsafed to them a far greater blessing than he has done of late. There have been more incoherent dreams than that in this world, and for this reason—first, *that which we have dreamed of is evidently needed.* Brethren, we are not amongst those who are prepared to croak and complain at the very first difficulty that may arise in a great enterprise, but no man can look upon our own Baptist Mission—and I suppose we are not much worse than others—without feeling that there is a pretty general flagging in missionary interest; and albeit that the funds may not much have fallen off, yet the annual recurrence of a debt, which is far from being welcome, together with other matters, goes to show that missionary zeal needs rekindling. This results partly from the fact that the novelty of the thing has gone off, the work having now been on the anvil for fifty years and more; and partly because we have had few very startling incidents of late to evoke a display of enthusiasm. That the missionary fire exists is certain, for when the recent events in Jamaica acted, as it were, as a refreshing breeze, the embers glowed and flamed anew. It is there, certainly, for the heart of the church is alive: it is there, but it is slumbering, somehow. You who recollect the thundering voice of William Knibb, and the great meetings which would be gathered when some such brethren returned home to tell what God had done amongst the heathen, must feel that you have fallen upon dull, uninteresting days in mission life; when the thing is flat and stale, and when men have reached the dregs of the wine, and the new wine is not in the cluster. Well, then, if it be so, let it be remembered that missionary zeal ought not to flag: if there be any one point in which the Christian church ought to keep its fervour at a white heat, it is concerning missions to the heathens. If there be anything about which we cannot tolerate lukewarmness, it is in the matter of sending the gospel to a dying world. How can we expect in such an enterprise, with difficulties to our poor weakness so insuperable, that we shall ever succeed if any of our strength be left unused? With all we have we are weak enough, but if we send but part of the army to the battle, if we exert but half of our strength, how can we expect that the blessing of God shall rest upon us? Depend upon it, that the flagging of zeal at home acts like a canker abroad, and when the heart of Christianity in England does not throb vigorously, every single limb of the missionary body feels the decline, and there is not a missionary anywhere, from the snows of Labrador to the burning heats of Africa, who is not enervated and injured when the Christian public at home begin to weary in well doing. It needs then, it imperatively needs, that our vision should be made a fact.

We may be excused our vision, because *it is very possible that it may be realised*. It is not a thing too hard to look for. It was far harder work, surely, to have established the mission than it will be most thoroughly and earnestly to revive it. If we will but enquire into what may have been the causes of any decline that exists, we shall not find them, I think, to be very deep, nor to be difficult of remedy; they are but superficial, and a little loving earnestness will soon remove them. Brethren, as a denomination, we are beginning to cluster more closely around our standard. We have been hitherto somewhat scattered over the field, isolated, divided, and therefore weak; but now we feel that our strength must lie, under God, in our unity, and our ranks are closing each man to his brother. We feel the fire of sacred love burning in our hearts, and as we come together, and begin to talk of the difficulties before us in a fraternal spirit, they will all vanish. Lovingly correcting errors, carefully removing excrescences, and boldly advancing, the stone shall be rolled away from the sepulchre before we reach it, or if not in God's name, and by his strength, we will roll it away ourselves; and if there has been a flagging, this very meeting, in which there are young and ardent spirits, shall help to supply the material with which to kindle a fire which shall nevermore grow dim.

More than that—it is not only possible that our dream may become a reality, *but it is very probable;* for so it always has been. If ever God's church has declined for a little while, unexpectedly there has been yielded a season of refreshing from the presence of the Lord. We know not what God has in store. He is great at surprises: his best wine last amazes us a" When the devil is most secure upon his throne, then God springs a mine, and blows his empire into atoms. Just when the wise virgins and the foolish alike have allowed their lamps to burn low, then is the cry heard, " Behold, the bridegroom cometh !" and those virgins arise and trim their lamps. So will it be among us. I am hopeful that, in answer to earnest prayer, God will speedily send amongst us a general intensity of desire for the glory of Christ, accompanied by breaking of heart and weeping of eye, for the perishing heathen, and a solemn resolve that, in Jehovah's strength we will spare no pains, and neglect no efforts, by which we may make the gospel known unto the ends of the earth. Yes, a thorough renovation of the missionary society, a resurrection of the mission spirit, and an arousing of our churches, is delightfully probable—it were wretched indeed if it were not so.

One thing more we will say upon this topic, namely, *that such a renewal is solemnly required of us.* What are our personal obligations to the Crucified? What owe we not to the gospel which has delivered us from an eternity of woe, and has guaranteed to us an everlasting career of blessedness? This night, redeemed, regenerated, adopted, justified, sanctified, with your feet upon the rock, a song in your mouth, and your goings established—will you not feel it to be a call from heaven, that you should be in earnest to gather in the Lord's chosen out of all nations that dwell upon the face of the earth? Did our Saviour slumber in his life-work? Was he tardy in his service for our redemption? Then might we grow lax; but if, setting his face to Jerusalem, he panted for the baptism wherein he was to be baptised, and was straitened until it was accomplished, then he claims of us, according to our measure, the same steadfastness of resolve, and perseverance of purpose, and sacrifice of self. I charge you, young men, as you have received Christ Jesus the Lord, be not slow to spend and be spent for him. All is too little, shall we give him less than all? Fervent services are too poor, shall we be lukewarm? Descend, O heavenly fire, and now inflame us, for less than thy flames cannot enable us to live as live we should!

I will not tarry upon this point. You have already forgiven me my dream.

II. LET US PROCEED TO ELABORATE THE VISION.

I was asked principally to address young men this evening. I am a young man myself, and, therefore, if I utter anything exceedingly visionary, you will observe its justification in the text, "Your young men shall see visions." My dream seemed to take this shape: *In order that missionary work should be reformed, revived, and carried on with energy and with hope of success, it seemed necessary that especially among our young members there should be a revival of intense and earnest prayer, and anxious sympathy with the missionary work.* The power of prayer can never be overrated. They who cannot serve God by preaching, need not regret it if they can be mighty in prayer. The true strength of the church lies there. This is the sinew which moves the arm of omnipotence. If a man can but pray, he can do anything. He that knows how to overcome the Lord in prayer, has heaven and earth at his disposal. There is nothing, man, which thou canst not accomplish if thou canst but prevail with God in prayer. Now, I will not say that we ought to have our prayer meetings for missionary objects more largely attended—everybody knows this, but does everybody try to attend? But I will say this, which is more likely to be forgotten, that it were well if we had settled private seasons of devotion, each of us, especially to intercede with God for the conversion of the heathen. It will be a notable day when the young men of this society say, "Not only will we attend the prayer meetings for this object, but we will, each one, as before the Lord, make it matter of conscience that there shall be at least one hour in the week sacredly hedged around and spent in private prayer for the missionary work." Beneath the banyan tree you will not stand, surrounded by black faces, and telling of Krishnu's Christ; but in your own little room, by the old arm-chair, you will as surely be bringing down showers of blessings upon the heathen by importunate entreaties. Here our old men and our matrons, as well as our young men and maidens, may unite. If it be so, that the entire church shall send up one impassioned, continuous, prevalent cry to God, "O Lord, make bare thine arm for Christ and for his truth!" verily, verily, I say unto you he shall avenge you speedily, though he bear long with you. Your prayers shall come up unto the ears of the Lord God of Sabaoth, and he will reveal the glory of his power.

Next, if our young men who see visions will *follow up their prayers with practical effort, then we shall see in our churches a larger and more efficient staff of collectors and contributors.* We should then find men who would give of their substance as a matter of principle, tithing themselves, or in other fair proportion, so that the kingdom of Christ should never have an empty exchequer. I speak to some who sit often in this place, who need not to have a word said to them by way of stirring them up to liberality, for I can glory in them in this respect, that they do beyond all that I could expect; but I wish that the same spirit of giving were paramount throughout all the church: that men would give, not because they are asked, nor by way of emulation or compulsion, but because God has given to them, and they recognise their stewardship. A few men in a church may often move the whole to liberality. The example of a few, and those few, perhaps, not the richest, may be contagious to the whole mass; and a few earnest young people especially, may often push right and left, with their proverbial enthusiasm, till they have stirred the inert mass, and constrained the whole body to be liberal to the cause of Jesus Christ.

Up till now my dream has been reasonable, you will say. I will now be more visionary. If we were all praying for missions, and all giving for their support, it might be very well asked of us, "What do ye more than others?" for what Romanist is there who is not zealous for the spread of his religion? What heathen is there who does not give quite as much as any of us give, ay, and a great deal more than we give, to his superstitions? But, supposing next to this, that there should be a number of young men here who know each other very well; young men who have been trained in the same sanctuary, nurtured in the same church, who should meet together to-morrow, or at such other time as shall be convenient, and say to one another, "Now, we are in business, we have just commenced in life, and God is prospering us, more or less; we are taking to ourselves wives; our children are coming around us; but still, we trust we are never going to permit ourselves to be swallowed up in a mere worldly way of living; now, what ought we to do for missions?" And suppose the enquiry should be put, "Is there one amongst us who could devote himself to go and teach the heathen for us? As we, most of us, may not have the ability, or do not feel called to the work, is there one out of twelve of us young men, who have grown side by side in the Sunday-school, who has the ability and who feels called to go? Let us make it a matter of prayer, and when the Holy Ghost saith, 'Separate So-and-So to the work,' then we, the other eleven who remain, will do this—we will say to him, 'Now, brother, you cannot stop at home to make your fortune or to earn a competence; you are now giving yourself up to a very arduous and earnest enterprise, and we will support you; we know you—we have confidence in you; you go down into the pit, we will hold the rope; go forth in connection with our own denominational society, but we will bear the expense year by year among ourselves! Have you faith enough to go trusting that the Lord will provide? Then, we will have faith enough, and generosity enough, to say that your wants shall be our care; you preach for Christ, we will make money for Christ; when you open the Bible for Christ, we will be taking down the shop shutters for Christ; and while you are unfolding the banner of Christ's love, we will be unfolding the calicos, or selling the groceries, and we pledge ourselves always to set aside your portion, because, as our brother, you are doing our work.'" I wish we had such godly clubs as these—holy confederacies of earnest young men who thus would love their missionary, feel for him, hear from him continually, and undertake to supply his support. Why, on such a plan as that, I should think, they would give fifty times, a hundred times, as much as ever they are likely to give to an impersonal society, or to a man whose name they only know, but whose face they never saw. I wonder whether I shall ever live to see a club of that kind? I wonder whether such a club will ever spring up in the midst of this church, or any of the churches in London? If it shall be so, I shall be glad to have seen a vision of it.

Further, I have dreamed also that there would spring up in our churches a very large number of young men who would count it to be the very highest ambition of their lives to give themselves up to the work of Jesus Christ abroad, and who, seeing that in London, and throughout England, men may hear the gospel if they will, while many of the heathen cannot hear it, like or no, would feel it to be their duty to serve Christ in the foreign field; and I have wondered whether we should have these noble fellows coming by the score, and saying, " Here am I, send me." Then I have considered whether God would pour out enough of the missionary spirit upon these men to make them say, " Well, the missionary society is in debt, and cannot take us: it has enough men to support already; it is doing a good work enough, I will not interfere with it; I do not want to be a burden to any brethren: will you send me out, and let me exercise my faith in God, only having this for my comfort, that you will stand at my back and give me what you can, while I will only draw upon you for what I cannot get for myself"? I wonder whether we shall see fifty or a hundred missionaries within the next year or two leaving our shores, whose passage has been paid, and who will land in some foreign country with just enough about them to keep them till the language has been learned, and who will then, in confidence in God, set about working to support themselves? I set Paul before you, young men. When he preached the gospel at the first, he was a tent-maker, and he earned his own living. Are there no occupations in these days by which a man may earn his living, and yet preach the gospel? It is not the best thing to do—the best thing is for a man to give all his time to his ministry; but if you cannot have the best, you must have the second best. Are there not to be found physicians who, in China and in India, would not only procure a sub-sistence, but much more, and might proclaim the gospel at the same time? Thank God there is such a thing as a medical mission! Thank God that the profession of medicine has not been behind in sending heroes to the field! But are there no other occupations? Young men, are there no clerkships to be had in India? I find men going out there by scores, to make their fortunes, and ruin their constitutions; and I see young women going out to get married to Indian settlers almost on speculation. Have we no young men and women who will go across the line, and find their way round the Cape of Good Hope, to preach the gospel, intending to use their commercial pursuits as a means of introduction and support? Surely it must be so. I know that at this present moment there are hundreds of Christian men living along the coasts of South America, especially of the Brazils, and the Argentine Republic, where skilled artisans, engineers, and such like, are in constant request by the government, and I have often hoped to hear that some of these men were originating Christian missions. I have often wondered why more has not been done of that kind. We hear of our young brethren going forth to Morocco, to Algiers, to Turkey, and Egypt—they are in demand in almost every part of the earth, for the young men of England are the very pick and prime of humanity; and the various trades which are connected with machinery are scarcely to be taught except by their means. What about their faith if they do not become evangelists? O young men and women, what grand opportunities must open up before some of you! I am sure they must, and if you did but set your hearts to it with a full resolve that you would not live the dead-and-alive life of most of us, but would distinguish yourselves in Christ's service, what might you not achieve! If there were a will, there would be a way; and if there were a fixed purpose, God would send the means; and he who quickened you to such a degree of spiritual life that you could not rest unless you were telling the gospel to the ungodly, would not let his providence so go athwart his grace as to shut the door in your face when you were willing to be serviceable to his cause.

"That is a dream," says one. Well, may some of you dream it, and in the midst of the dream may there rise up before you a face which, as it shall by degrees settle and become clear, and you shall discern its features, shall be wonderfully like your own, and as you wake may you have to say, "Here am I, Lord, send me, for whithersoever thou wouldst have me go, there will I go, to proclaim the name and the love of our Lord Jesus Christ."

Oh! when shall I see once again the missionary going from door to door, determined, according to his Master's command, that whatsoever things they set before him he will eat, believing that the labourer is worthy of his hire, and that he is to expect to find his hire amongst those to whom he preaches the gospel; believing that the acceptance of hospitality is the master-key of missions, and that the eating of the strangers' salt is the nearest way to put before them the bread of life, and the reception of hospitable courtesy the very stepping-stone towards the giving out of the precious gospel? May we live to see this! We shall, by God's grace, if his Spirit visits us.

III. Lastly, and but very briefly, what shall we do to assist THE REALISATION OF THIS VISION?

We can all do something if we love the Lord, and that something will be eminently a blessing to ourselves. If ever we are to see the missionary spirit brought to its very highest and most perfect condition, *it must be by each individual's own personal piety mounting to the very highest degree of elevation.* Why, we are not half saints—we seem, many of us, to forget what sainthood means; we are content to be just saved, like the drowning man dragged to shore just alive, and that is all. O that we were not satisfied with this, but that our love to Christ were flaming, our hope in Jesus Christ bright and clear, our faith in God firm and unstaggering. O that we served Christ, not at a snail's pace, but with the utmost energy of the best conditioned manhood. O that we loved Christ and worked for Christ up to the last ounce at which the engine could be driven! O that we could but just for once see what manhood could do when God was in it. O that some of us were raised up to be as Brainerd, living, dying, through love to Christ; men who were conquered by divine love, led in fetters as slaves to the blessed captivity of love to the souls of men. May it grow into a passion with you, men and women, to snatch fire-brands from the flame! You will never be very useful until it is so. If holy work be a mere diversion for your leisure moments, you will do nothing; you must make a trade of it, a solemn occupation of it. It must be your calling, your meat, and your drink, to do the will of him that sent you. When the Christian church glows in this fashion, it will swell with an intense heat like a volcano, whose tremendous furnaces cannot be contained within itself, but its sides begin to move and bulge, and then after a rumbling and a heaving, a mighty sheet of fire shoots right up to heaven, and afterwards streams of flaming lava run from its red lips down, burning their way along the plain beneath. Oh! to get such a fire for God's cause into the heart of the Christian church, till she began to heave and throb with unquenchable emotion, and then a mighty sheet of the fire-prayer should go up towards heaven, and afterwards the burning lava of her all-conquering zeal should flow over all lands, till all nations should enquire, " What is this new thing in the earth, and what this modern miracle, and what this cross of Christ for which men live and die?"

I would say, as subsidiary to this great thing—which is the main matter-to-night—*that young men and young women would do well to feed the flame of their zeal with greater information as to the condition of the world in reference to our mission-work.* I wish that those who supply us with our periodical missionary literature had any idea of the great difficulty there is in keeping awake while reading it. I should be glad if they could by any means put a small allowance of salt into it, or serve it up in a more tempting form. I do not plead for making it into light literature, far from it, but if our editors could anyhow give us something that would tempt the literary or the spiritual palate, it would be well. But, young men, you are not dependent upon periodical literature—I almost regret that there is such a thing—there are solid books to be got at. There are libraries teeming with the works of missionaries—their travels, their adventures; the history of heathen nations—their desolations, their wants, their crimes, their idolatries, their infamies. There is a great literature for you. You may not have time to get through it all, but if you read some of it, I think you will feel a great accession to your zeal.

When you have gained such information, which may be as fuel to the fire, I pray you *keep yourselves right in this matter by constant, energetic efforts in connection with works at home.* Those who do not serve God at home, are of no use anywhere. It is all very well to talk about what you would do if you could speak to the Hindoos. Nonsense! what do you do when you are in the streets of Whitechapel? You will be of no use whatever in Calcutta, unless you are of use in Poplar or Bermondsey. The human mind is the same everywhere. Its sins may take another form, but there are just the same difficulties in one place as in another. It is all very well for you to turn a sort of Don Quixote in imagination, and dream of what you would do if you went out upon a spiritual crusade as a heavenly knight-errant, tilting against windmills; just try your hand at the conversion of that young man who sits next you in the pew. See what you can do for Jesus Christ in the shop. See whether you can serve your Master in that little Bible-class of which you are a member. Rest assured that no missionary ardour really burns in the breast of that man who does not love the souls of those who live in the same house and dwell in the same neighbourhood. Give me that man for a missionary of whom it is said, that when he took a lodging in a house, all the other inhabitants were brought to God within six months; or he was a son, and his father was unconverted, but he gave the Lord no rest till he saw his parent saved; or he was a tradesman, and while he was pushing his business earnestly, he always found time to be an evangelist. That is the man who will maintain missionary fervour alive at home, and that is the man who will help to promote missionary effort abroad.

Brethren and sisters, these are the practical points: have a higher degree of piety, a wider and more extensive knowledge, and a more practical zeal in God's work near to your hand.

But oh! do make sure that you are saved yourselves. Do make sure that you yourselves know the Christ whom you profess to teach. That missionary-box, what is it but an infamous sham if you put into it **your** offering, but withhold your heart? You talk about missionary collecting, missionary meetings, lectures to the young, and I know not what, when you yourself are a stranger to the power of vital godliness! No, my dear friend; begin at home. May the Lord begin with you. O young men, young women, are you yet unsaved? Then instead of your pitying the heathen, the heathen may well pity you! How might a heathen with a tender heart stand here and say, "If that Bible be true, if that gospel which you talk of has really come from God, if Christ be the Saviour, if there be no salvation out of him, then how I pity you who have heard about it and yet have rejected it! How I pity you, because your own Saviour, whom you profess to serve, out of his own mouth of love has said it, that it shall be more tolerable for Sodom and Gomorrha in the day of judgment than for you!" Oh! then, let it be to-night that you give your heart to God, and when you have given your heart to him, then think of the matter of which I have spoken.

God grant that my vision may become a fact. May you help to make it so, and Christ shall have the glory. Amen.

2   Unto You, Young Men

"I have written unto you, young men, because ye are strong, and the word of God abideth in you, and ye have overcome the wicked one."—1 John ii. 14.

JOHN abounded in charity, but with the utmost stretch of it he could not have written to all young men in this style, for, alas! all young men are not strong, nor doth the word of God abide in them all, nor have they all overcome the wicked one.   Strong in muscle they may be, like Samson, but like Samson they are weak in moral principle, and ere long are found in the lap of a sinful Delilah, to their own destruction.   What multitudes of young men there are in London who, instead of being spiritually strong, are weakness itself—bending like the willow in every gale, drifting down the stream like dead fish, having neither the wish nor the ability to stem the torrent of temptation!   These weak young men, who are entrapped in every snare, taken with every bait, are the objects of our earnest anxiety ; but to them we can address no epistles entreating their aid in holy work, or cheering them with sacred consolatious.

It is painful to reflect that in the vast mass of ripening manhood the word of God does *not* abide.   Tens of thousands of them do not even hear it.   They look upon the Sabbath as a day of amusement, and to religious exercises as a slavery.   Thousands more attend to the word only after the fashion of the old proverb, " In at one ear and out at the other."   They see their natural face in the glass of the word, but they go their way and straightway forget what manner of men they are. They are young men of good judgment, too, in worldly things, and yet so foolish as to esteem eternal things as mere trifles, to play with immortality, and to value the joys of an hour at a higher price than bliss unending.

Assuredly in this land there are multitudes of young men who have not overcome the wicked one.   Nay, they never thought of so doing, for they are hand in glove with him—they are among his best allies. Shame that it should be so, that when the devil seeks recruits for his army, he should straightway send his recruiting sergeant for these fine young fellows, who ought to serve a better master, but who are all too willing to give up at once the strength of their youth and the force of

No. 811.

their characters to the service of a deceiver—overcome the wicked one, indeed! In many young men he reigns supreme, and they are led captive by him at his will; wickedly insinuating all the while that they are the milksops and the fools who dare to do the right and scorn to to fling away their souls for the sake of temporary pleasures.

Now, there may be in this place to-night some of these young men who are not strong, in whom the word of God does not abide, and who have not overcome the wicked one. Let conscience seek out such, and when they are fully revealed and discovered to themselves, let them deliberately take stock of their position in the light of death and judgment, and may they by God's grace be made to pause awhile, and then to decide that it will be a wiser course of action to repent before God, to believe in Jesus, and to give themselves up to him who can make them strong, and put the living seed of his word into their hearts, and enable them to overcome the wicked one.

But I address myself to many, I trust, this evening, who are such as John described, and who can give praise to distinguishing grace that they are such, for they feel that had they been left to themselves they would have possessed no strength, and would not have held the living truth within their hearts. O for a shout of sacred joy from every one who has been redeemed from his estate of bondage, brought up out of the wilderness, and led into the Canaan of salvation! O for something better than shouts of praise, namely, holy lives, devoted actions, constant consecration, from those who thus have been strengthened and quickened, and made victors over sin.

Two or three things we shall speak about to-night. First, *our text describes the model young man;* secondly, we infer from it *that such model men have within them qualifications for usefulness.* John wrote to these young men because they were so-and-so, and so-and-so. I shall ask some here to serve God for the selfsame reason, because those parts which make the model man are just such as will qualify them to serve God; and, in the third and last place, *I shall try to urge the conscription upon many here*, hoping that many will be written down as God's warriors from this good hour.

I. First, then, we have before us THE PHOTOGRAPH OF THE MODEL YOUNG MAN.

Nothing is said about his learning—he may be a model of everything that is spiritually good though his education may have been neglected; nothing is said about his wealth, his position in society, or his personal appearance: without anything to boast of in relation to any of these things he may yet be in the advance guard of Christ's soldiers.

1. What is spoken in the text has to do only with spiritual qualifications, and it deals with three points. First, *this young man is strong.* The strength here meant is, not that which is the *result* of his being in his youth—not a mere natural vigour, but a spiritual strength, a strength which cometh of the Lord of hosts, a strength which is the result of the indwelling of the Spirit within the man; a strength which brings out and consecrates the natural energy, and makes the young man with his vigour to be vigorous in the right direction. "I have written unto you, young men, because ye are strong."

Now, the spiritually strong man may be described in this way—*he is one who is very decided for Christ.* He is not half-hearted, halting between two opinions. There is nothing about him now, as there once might have been, of questioning or hesitation. He is for Christ. Whoever may be for the false, he is for the true. Whoever may side with the unjust, he is for the honest. Whoever may adopt crooked policy, he is for straightforward principle. He has made up his mind to it, that he is Christ's, and henceforth he does not tolerate within his soul anything like a question on that matter. He is decided, not only in his service of Christ, but in his opinions. He knows what he knows. He holds firmly what he does hold. He is a strong man in the truth. You cannot pull him by the ear this way to-day and that way to-morrow. He does not depend upon his religious teacher for his religious thought; he does his own thinking with-his Bible before him: by the grace of God he has grown strong by feeding on heavenly diet. He is a man with his feet firmly planted on a rock. You may meet with weak professors almost everywhere, and you may by specious arguments entice them to almost everything, but the young man who is strong will listen to what you have to say, and weigh it in the scales of judgment, but when once weighed and found wanting, he will reject it without hesitation. He at once rejects the wrong, and cleaves to that which is right, for God has made him strong in integrity of heart.

While thus strong in decision, *he is also strong in the matter of establishment.* He once believed truths because he was so taught, but now he begins to search to the roots of them, and to find out the arguments which support them. He has proved, if not all things, yet enough to hold fast that which is good. He has become established by some little experience, for, though a young man, experience may come to him, and, indeed, it does come to some young men without the lapse of many years. The experience of a single night has taught a man more than the experience of years, and the experience of a single day, a bitter sorrow, or ardent labour, has been more valuable than the mere lapse of a score of ordinary years of prosperity and joy. What little experience the man has had, and what little observation he has been able to make, have joined together to confirm him in what he believes; and now, though he does not care to be always arguing—in fact, he has passed beyond that stage; though he does not care to be always testing and trying things—he has advanced farther than that —yet he is prepared, when objections are advanced, to meet them in a spirit of meekness, and he is prepared to instruct the ignorant, and those who are out of the way. He is strong in establishment, as well as in decision. Nor is this all. He has become strong, through the grace of our Lord Jesus Christ, *in a vigour diffused throughout his whole spiritual constitution.* A very large proportion of the members of our churches are, I trust, alive, but you have to try them by various experiments to know whether there is any life in them. They are like persons just fished up from the water, and in order to discover whether they are alive, you place the looking-glass before their mouth and watch for a little damp upon it; you kneel down and try to detect the faint sound of breathing.

> " 'Tis a point I long to know,
> Oft it causes anxious thought,"

This is the miserable cry of many. There may be life in them, but it is life in a fainting fit or sound sleep. But the vigorous Christian is far different from this. He does not ask whether he is alive or not; he knows he is, by that which he is enabled to do, by the strength of his life; by that which he feels palpitating within; by the aspirations that glow within his soul; ay, and even by the griefs and pains which make him bow his head. He *knows* that he lives. Others in our churches do something for Christ, and know that they are alive, but their whole spiritual system is relaxed. If they take up the hammer and work for God, they strike such feeble blows that the nails do not know it. If they take the spade in their hand to dig in the Master's vineyard, the weeds laugh them to scorn. They are so exceedingly feeble, and generally so changeable, so fond of new work, and of running after this and that, that they are of little or no real service to the church. But the strong man in Christ Jesus is one who, if he fights, dashes to pieces the helmet of his foe; and if he wields the sling and the stone, takes care that the stone shall be sent with force enough to go through Goliath's skull. He is a man who, if he prays, makes the gates of heaven shake and the vaults of heaven to ring. He is a man who, when he pleads with sinners, pleads all over—hands and face, and every muscle revealing his earnestness. He cannot drag on a dead-and-alive life. He feels that if religion be worth anything it is worth everything, and he throws his whole being into it—body, soul, and spirit, ardently and to the utmost pitch of energy, being given up to the Master's cause.

Meanwhile, he is not only strong in actual service, but *he is strong in what he cannot do.* Some of the most acceptable things which are recorded in heaven are the things which are in our hearts, but which cannot come to our hands for want of power. It is a great thing, brethren, always to have some work before you which makes you stand on tip-toe to reach it, and to be continually reaching up till at last you attain it, and then reach to something still beyond you. I like the thought of David sitting down before the Lord, and meditating about that house of cedar which he was not permitted to build. The strong young man will have many schemes crossing his brain, and while he is in his youth he will not be able to realise them, but they will flit before him so often, that at last he will pluck up courage, and as he grows in years and possibilities, he will at last make real that which once was but a dream. Do not be ashamed, my dear young friend, you who have scarcely left your father's roof, do not be ashamed sometimes to have a few right thorough day-dreams, do not be ashamed to indulge in thoughts of what you would do if you could. I say this provided that you are now doing all you can, and this day consecrating to God all you have. Go to him, and ask him to enable you to do more in your future life, and plan and purpose for that future life; have a strength of purpose, and it may be, God will give you strength of opportunity, and if he do not, yet it shall be well that it was in your heart. I may say, too, even in the presence of the honoured fathers who surround the pulpit, we sadly want a generation of stronger men in our churches. We will not decry the blessings which God has given us already. I do not believe that any age was better than this, all things considered, but this is the time when we shall want our young men to be strong to all the intents of strength. Battles are coming in which they will need to stand with firm foot. There will be strifes in which they will not be of the slightest value if they cannot brave the conflict in the very van, or fight where fly whole showers of fiery arrows and hot bolts of hell. Rest assured these are not silken days, nor times to make us dream that we have won the victory. Our fathers, where are they? They are looking down upon us from their thrones, but what do they see? Do they see us wearing the crown and waving the palm-branch? If so, they see us lunatics indeed, for that were a madman's sport; but rather they see us sharpening our swords afresh, and buckling on our panoply anew, to fight the same fight which they fought under other circumstances. The young blood of the church, under God, is our great hope in the conflict for King Jesus. The young men of the church must be in the next twenty years the very soul and vigour of it, and therefore, may God raise up among us a goodly seed, a race of heroes, swifter than eagles for zeal, and stronger than lions for faith.

2. The text gives a further description of the model Christian young man in the words, "*And the word of God abideth in you.*" Her Majesty was on the south side of the water to-day, but she does not abide there. All the pomp and sunshine of her presence have vanished, and Westminster Bridge and Stangate are as they were before. The word of God sometimes comes with right royal pomp into the minds of young men; they are affected by it for a time, and they rejoice therein, but, alas! that blessed word soon departs, and they are none the better for that which they have heard. Multitudes still are stony-ground hearers; they receive the word with joy, but they have no root, and by-and-by they all wither away. The model young man in the text is not of this kind. The word of God abideth in him, by which I understand that *he is one who understands the word*, for it must get into him before it can abide in him, and it can only enter by the door of the understanding: he understands the word, and then by having an affection for the word he shuts to that door and entertains the truth. Men who understand the gospel are not quite so common as we sometimes suppose. I am not certain whether the giving up of the use of the *Westminster Assembly's Catechism* was a very wise thing. That grand old epitome of doctrine conveys to those who are taught it intelligently a most solid basis upon which afterwards the truth may be built. A considerable number of our church members do not understand the truth which they profess to have received. I believe this is more or less true of all denominations, and that the pastors need to adopt measures, by classes or otherwise, which, under the Holy Spirit's blessing, might build up our youth in our most holy faith. The model young man is thus taught; he understands the truth so far as it is a matter of intellect; he grapples it to himself as with hooks of steel by intense affection, and then he lives it out with all his soul: while he holds the word of God as a doctrine, it holds him as a living indwelling force.

The word of God abides in him, that is, *he is constantly feeling its effects*. It abides in him, " a well of water springing up unto everlasting life "—a sacred fire consuming his sins, and comforting his spirit. It abides in him, a heavenly messenger revealing to him the freshness of celestial truth, uplifting him from earthly desires, and preparing him for the mansions in the skies. The gospel permeates his nature. It is intertwisted into his very self. You would more readily destroy him than make him apostatise.

> "The cords that bind around his heart
> Tortures and riches might tear off;
> But they could never, never part
> The hold he has on Christ his Lord."

The word of God has become God's resident lieutenant, dwelling in his spirit, reigning like a sovereign over his entire soul. It abides within him as an incorruptible seed, which death itself cannot kill. This is the blessed young man indeed, God has blessed him, and who shall reverse the benediction?

3. Thirdly, the text adds, "*And ye have overcome the wicked one.*" This is said of the young man. He is but a young man in grace; he has not reached the point of fatherhood in Christ, but for all that he has overcome the wicked one. It strikes me that Christianity used aforetime to be spoken of as a more effective thing than it is now. When people pray they seldom speak positively about what religion has done for them. I have often heard a brother say, "The Lord has done great things for us: whereof *we desire* to be glad." Why, dear brother, if the Lord has done great things for you, you *are* glad. I have known that text, "The love of Christ constraineth us," preached from as if it said that the love of Christ *ought* to constrain us—which is very true, but it is not the truth of the text. It *does* constrain us; it does rule in the soul. We often speak of wrestling with Satan, struggling and striving to overcome; but the text speaks of a victory already achieved, and too, by young men. We dishonour God, and make people think little of the gospel, when we put in those pretendedly humbling terms, which are only used to let people see how exceedingly humble we are. We are so mock modest as to refuse to acknowledge the power of divine grace in our own souls. As a man, I would speak diffidently about anything that I do myself, but of anything that God has done in me, or for me, or by me, I shall not speak with bated breath, but affirm it and rejoice in it, that God may be glorified thereby.

There are men here who have overcome the devil, and they have overcome him in many shapes. There are many pictures of the devil about, but I am afraid there are none of them accurate, for he assumes different shapes in different places. He is a chameleon, always affected by the light in which he happens to be; a Proteus, assuming every shape, so that it may but subserve his purpose. Some young men have overcome that blue devil which keeps men despairing, doubting, trembling, and fearing. You once were subject to him. You could not, you said, believe in Christ. You were afraid you never should be saved. You wrote bitter things against yourself. Ah! but you have cast him out now by a simple faith in Jesus; for you know whom you have believed, and you are persuaded that he is able to keep that which you have committed unto him. You have overcome that devil, and though he does try to come back, and when your business is a little troublesome, or the liver may not be acting properly, he endeavours to insinuate himself, yet by God's grace, he shall never fasten on the old chains again.

Then there is that dust-eating devil, of whom we can never speak too badly—the yellow devil of the mammon of unrighteousness, the love of gold and silver; the dread god of London, rolling over this city as if it were all his own. I think I see him as a dragon on the top of the church steeple, chuckling at the inscription over the Royal Exchange—"The earth is the Lord's, and the fulness thereof," and laughing because he knows better, for he reckons it all belongs to him; even as of old he said to Christ, "All these things will I give thee, if thou wilt fall down and worship me." What tricks are done nowadays in business for the love of gold! In fact, we know, some of us who are not business men, but who, nevertheless, are not blind, that dishonest marks and dishonest measures have become so systematic that their effect is lost, and the thing itself is almost as honest as if it were honest. It is the fact that men have become so accustomed to say that twice three make seven that their neighbours all say, "Exactly so, and we will pay you for the goods after the same reckoning," so that the thing has to square itself. But the genuine Christian, the man who is strong, and has the word of God abiding in him, scorns all this. He hears others say, "We must live," but he replies, "Yes, but we must die." He determines that he will not throw away his soul in order to grasp wealth, and that if it be not possible to become a merchant prince without the violation of the code of honour and of Christ's law, then he will be content to be poor. O young man, if you have come to this you have overcome a wicked one indeed! I am afraid there are some here with gray heads who have hardly ventured on the fight. Alas! for them.

Another form of the wicked one we must speak of but softly, but oh! how hard to be overcome by the young man, I mean Madam Wanton, that fair but foul, that smiling but murderous fiend of hell, by whom so many are deluded. Solomon spake, "of the strange woman," but the strong Christian in whom the word of God abides, passes by her door and shuts his ear to her siren song. He flees youthful lusts which war against the soul, he reserves both his body and his soul for his Lord who has redeemed him by his precious blood.

Young man, if you are strong, and have overcome the wicked one, you have overcome, I trust, *that Lucifer of pride*, and it is your endeavour to walk humbly with your God! You have given up all idea of merit. You cannot boast nor exalt yourself, but you bow humbly at the foot of the cross, adoring him who has saved you from the wrath to come.

You have given up also, I trust, young man, all subjection to the great red dragon *of fashion*, who draws with his tail even the very stars of heaven. There are some who would think it far worse to be considered unfashionable than to be thought unchristian. To be unchristian would be but such a common accusation that they might submit to it; but to be unfashionable would be horrible indeed! Young men in London get to be affected by this. If the young men in the house are going to such-and-such an entertainment—they all read a certain class of books—if they are dissipated and sceptical, then the temptation is to chime in with them, and only the man who is

strong, and hath the word of God abiding in him, will overcome the
wicked one by doing the right alone—

"Faithful among the faithless found."

II. Thus I have described a model Christian young man. Let us
further observe that THESE THINGS WHICH CONSTITUTE HIM WHAT HE IS
ARE HIS QUALIFICATIONS FOR USEFULNESS.

Of course, certain talents are necessary for certain positions, but it is
a rule without exception that every child of God may be useful in the
divine family. God has not one single servant for whom he has not
appointed a service. Now, observe, my friends, to whom I am now
addressing myself—you are strong: granted that, then this very
strength which you now have will enable you to do mission-work for
God, and the graces which have been wrought in you, through Christ
Jesus, faith, love, courage, patience, are your fitnesses for sacred labour.

If you are to be a minister, you may need to acquire a measure of
learning; if you are to be a missionary, you will need a peculiar
training, but you can get these; God will give you strength to obtain
them, and the spiritual strength will go very far to help you. Meanwhile,
for other work, all the strength you require is that which you already
possess. There are persons in the world who will not let us speak a
word to the unconverted, because they say, and say very truly, that unconverted men are dead in sin, and therefore we are not to tell them to
live, because they have no power to live. They forget that we have the
power in the quickening word and Spirit of God, and that as we speak
the word for God, power goes with it. Now, there is among us too much
of this forgetfulness of the fact, that we actually have power from on
high. In prayer we are always praying for the outpouring of the Holy
Spirit, which is very proper; but, remember, we have the Holy Spirit—
the spirit *is* here. He is not always manifest, but he is given to his
church to abide in every one of his people, and if we would but believe
in his presence we should feel it more. They who preach most
successfully will tell you that one cause of it is that they *expect* to be
successful. They do not preach hoping that perhaps one or two may
be saved, but *knowing* that they will be, because the word of God is the
power of God unto salvation. They believe in the Holy Ghost, and
they who do so see the Holy Ghost, but they who only waveringly hope
in the Holy Ghost, discern him not: according to their faith so is it
unto them. Believe, my brother, that you have within you, as a believer,
the power which is necessary for reforming that house of business
of yours, which is now so godless, into a house of prayer. Believe it,
and begin to work like those who do believe it. Believe that those who
pass you in the morning, my young artisan friend, may be and shall be
converted by you and by God if you speak to them out of your heart.
Go up to them as one who knows that God is working with him; they
will be awed by your manner, and if they reject your message they will
feel it go hard with their consciences.

"I write unto you, young men, for ye are strong." We beg you to
use that strength in winning souls for Christ. Remember that this
very strength which brings a blessing to yourself will benefit another.
That very faith which brought you to Christ is all you want to bring

others to Christ. "He seeing *their* faith, said unto the sick of the palsy, Thy sins be forgiven thee." You shall find that wherein you are weak spiritually within, you will be powerless spiritually without for Christian service; and in as far as you are strong within for your personal communion with the Lord Jesus, to that extent shall you be strong without for the work of your Lord. Arise, ye strong young men; ye who saw the face of Christ this morning in your closets; ye who have waited upon him in prayer during the day; ye that delight in his word, arise, and shake yourselves from the dust! Be active in the might which God has given you to serve him while yet you may. As the angel said to Gideon, so say I to you, young man, "The Lord is with thee, thou mighty man of valour;" and yet, again, "Go in this thy strength."

If the young man enquires for tools and weapons with which to serve his Master, we refer him to the next point in the text, *"The word of God abideth in you."* Now, my dear brother, if you desire to teach others, you have not to ask what the lesson shall be, for it abides in you. Do you want a text that will impress the careless? What impressed you? You cannot have a better. You desire to speak a word in season from the word of God which shall be likely to comfort the disconsolate. What has comforted your own soul? You cannot have a better guide. You have within your own experience a tutor which cannot fail you, and you have also an encouragement that cannot be taken from you. The word of God within you will well up like a spring; and truth and grace will pour forth from you in rivers. I have heard our Lord likened to a man carrying a water-pot, and as he carried it upon his shoulder, the water fell dropping, dropping, dropping, so that every one could track the water-bearer. So should all his people be, carrying such a fulness of grace that every one should know where they have been by that which they have left behind. He who hath lain in the beds of spices will perfume the air through which he walks. One who, like Asher, has dipped his foot in oil, will leave his footprints behind him. When the living and incorruptible seed remains within, the divine instincts of the new nature will guide you to the wisest methods of activity. You will do the right thing under the inward impulse rather than the written law, and your personal salvation will be your prime qualification for seeking out others of your Master's flock.

Once again, *" you have overcome the wicked one."* The man who has once given Satan a slap in the face need not be afraid of men. If you have often stood foot to foot with a violent temptation, and, after wrestling, have overcome it, you can laugh to scorn all the puny adversaries who assail you. It will breed manliness within the young man, and make him a truly muscular Christian to have been practised in inward conflicts. *You* have overcome Satan by the power of grace—*you;* why, then there is hope that in the Sunday-school class which you have to teach, in the hearts of those boys and girls, Satan may again be conquered. There is hope for that drunken man you have been talking with lately; why should not he overcome the wicked one? You were once weak enough, but grace has made you strong: what grace has done for you it can do for another. "After I was saved myself," said one, "I never despaired of any other." So should the fact that you have been enabled to achieve a conquest in a very terrible strife, comfort you with regard to all other cases. Go into the back slums—they are not far off; penetrate the dark lanes and alleys. You have overcome the wicked one; you cannot meet with anything worse than him whom you have already vanquished. Let the majesty of grace in your souls be to you a solace and a stimulus, and never say anything is too hard for you to do who have already met Apollyon face to face and put him to the rout.

III. The wording of the text suggested to me, TO FORCE THE CONSCRIPTION. "*I have written unto you, young men.*"

In the French wars, certain young men, unhappily, found their names written down in the conscription, and were marched to the wars. Now, in a war from which none of us desire to escape, I hope there are young men here to-night whose names are written down—heavenly conscripts—who are summoned to-night, more fully than ever before in their lives, to go forth to the battle of the Lord of Hosts. I invite every young man here who is already converted to God, to dedicate himself to the Lord Jesus Christ to-night. It is not a matter that I can talk you into, nor indeed would I try it, but I would ask you to sit still a moment, and consider with yourselves this: " I am a believer in Christ; I have been lately to the sacramental table; I profess to have been chosen of God, to have been redeemed with precious blood, to have been separated from the rest of mankind, to be destined for an immortality most brilliant: am I living as becometh a redeemed one?" Passing your hand over your brow thoughtfully, you will come to the conclusion, probably, " I am not; I am serving God, I trust, in a way, but not with all my heart, and soul, and strength, as I should. How about my time ? Do I devote as much of that as I can to sacred work? How about my talent? Does that display itself most in the Literary Association or in the Sabbath-school? Are my oratorical abilities most developed in the debating room or in preaching at the street corner? Am I giving to Christ the prime, and choice, and vigour of my life? If I am not, I ought to do so; I ought, I feel I ought, to be altogether Christ's; not that I should leave my business, but I must make my business Christ's business, and so conduct it, and so to distribute of its results, as to prove that I am Christ's steward, working in the world for him, and not for self. Dear friends, if this night you shall not so much vow as pray that from this time there shall not be a drop of blood in your body, nor a hair of your head, nor a penny in your purse, nor a word on your tongue, nor a thought in your heart, but what shall be altogether the Lord's, I shall be glad enough.

It will be well if you take a step further as conscripts. You "holy work-folk"—as they used to call those who dwelt around the cathedral at Durham, and were exempt from all service to the baron because they served the church—I want you now *to think of some particular walk and department in which as young men and young women you can devote yourselves wholly to Christ.* Generalities in religion are always to be avoided, more especially generalities in service. If a man waits upon you for a situation, and you say to him, "What are you?" if he replies, "I am a painter, or a carpenter," you can find him work perhaps, but if he says, " Oh ! I can do anything," you understand that he can do nothing. So it is with a sort of spiritual jobbers who profess to be able to do anything in the church, but who really do nothing. I want my conscript brethren to-night to consider what they are henceforth going to do, and I beg them to consider it with such deliberation that when once they have come to a conclusion, that they will not need to change it, for changes involve losses. What can you do? What is your calling? Ragged schools? Sunday schools? Street preaching? Tract distribution? Here is a choice for you, which do you select? Waste no time, but say, "This is my calling, and by God's grace I will give myself up to it, meaning to do it as well as any man ever did do it—if possible, better; meaning if I take to the ragged school to be a thoroughly good teacher of those little Arabs; if I take to the Sunday school intending to make myself as efficient in the class as ever teacher could be." It shall be no small blessing to the churches whom you represent if such a resolve be made, and if the conscripts be found to-night of such a sort.

I would enquire next, *whether there may not be young men here who can give themselves up to the Christian ministry*, which is a step farther. There are many men who ought to be employed in the Christian ministry who stand back. You need not expect that you will gain earthly wealth by it. If you have any notion of that sort, I pray you keep to your breaking of stones; that will pay you better. If you have any idea that you will find the ministry an easy life, I entreat you to try the treadmill, for that would be an amusement compared with the life of the genuine Christian minister—in London, at least. But if you feel an intense earnestness to win souls, and if you have succeeded in speaking on other subjects, and can get some attention, think whether you cannot devote yourself to the work. Ah! young man, if I cast an ambitious thought into your mind I mean it only for my Master's glory. If the Lord should say to-night " Separate me Saul and Barnabas to this work," if he should call out some fine, noble young fellow, who might have given himself up, perhaps, to the pursuits of commerce, but who now will dedicate himself to the service of the Christian ministry, it would be well. Take care you keep not back whom God would have.

Then, further, I have to say, *may there not be here some young man who will become a conscript for missionary service abroad?* " I write unto you, young men, because ye are strong, and the word of God abideth in you, and ye have overcome the wicked one." *You* are the men we want. Dr. Mullens and Mr. Robinson will be glad to hear of you. I might to-night read a sort of proclamation such as I see sometimes issued by Her Majesty—" Wanted, young men." We give no description about the inches, either in girth or the height, but we do give this description—" Wanted, young men who are strong; in whom the word of God abideth, and who have overcome the wicked one." You who are weak had better stop at home in the Christian nursery a little while. You, in whom the word of God does not as yet abide, had need to stay till you be taught what be the elements of the faith. You, who have not overcome the wicked one, had better flesh your maiden swords in home fields of conflict. You are not the men who are wanted. But you who are strong enough to do and to dare for Jesus—you who are spiritually-minded enough to have overcome the monster of evil within yourselves—you are the men to fight Satan abroad, in his strongholds of heathendom, and Popery, and Mohammedanism. You, the choice men of the church, you are the men whom the Missionary Society requires. Think of it to-night before you go to sleep, and if the Lord incline you, come forward and say, "Here am I; send me."

Once again. If this be impossible, and I suppose it may be to the most of us, then *may we not get up a conscription to-night of young men who will resolve to help at home those who have the courage to go abroad?* You have nobly done, as young men, in endeavouring to raise a large sum for the work. You are an example to every Christian denomination in that respect. But do not let the project fall short of its full completion, and when it is completed take care that you do it again, for it is good to be zealous *always* in a good thing. We should forget the things that are behind, and press forward to that which is before. It will be a great thing when all Christian merchants do what some are doing, namely, give of their substance to the cause of Christ in due proportion. It is a blessed thing for a young man to begin business with the rule that he will give the Lord at least his tenth. That habit of weekly storing for Christ, and then giving to Christ out of his own bag instead of giving from your own purse is a most blessed one. Cultivate it, you young tradesmen who have just set up in business for yourselves, and you good wives, help your husbands to do it. You young men who are clerks, and have regular incomes, make that a regular part of your weekly business, and let some share of the consecrated spoil go to the Lord's foreign field. At the same time, never let your subscriptions to this or that act as an exoneration from personal service; give yourselves to Christ—your whole selves in the highest state of vigour, your whole selves constantly, intelligently, without admixture of sinister motives.

May God send his blessing, for Jesus' sake. Amen.

3 A Sermon for Young Men and Young Women

"Son of man, behold, they of the house of Israel say, The vision that he seeth is for many days to come, and he prophesieth of the times that are far off."—Ezekiel xii. 27.

ONE would have thought that if the glorious Lord condescended to send his servants to speak to men of the way of salvation, all mankind would delight to hear the message. We should naturally conclude that the people would immediately run together in eager crowds to catch every word, and would be obedient at once to the heavenly command. But, alas! it has not been so. Man's opposition to God is too deep, too stubborn for that. The prophets of old were compelled to cry, "Who hath believed our report?" and the servants of God in later times found themselves face to face with a stiff-necked generation, who resisted the Holy Ghost as did their fathers. Men display great ingenuity in making excuses for rejecting the message of God's love. They display marvellous skill, not in seeking salvation, but in fashioning reasons for refusing it; they are dexterous in avoiding grace, and in securing their own ruin. They hold up first this shield and then the other, to ward off the gracious arrows of the gospel of Jesus Christ, which are only meant to slay the deadly sins which lurk in their bosoms. The evil argument which is mentioned in the text has been used from Ezekiel's day right down to the present moment, and it has served Satan's turn in ten thousand cases. By its means men have delayed themselves into hell. The sons of men, when they hear of the great atonement made upon the cross by the Lord Jesus, and are bidden to lay hold upon eternal life in him, still say concerning the gospel, "The vision that he seeth is for many days to come, and he prophesieth of times that are far off." That is to say, they pretend that the matters whereof we speak are not of immediate importance, and may safely be postponed. They imagine that religion is for the weakness

of the dying and the infirmity of the aged, but not for healthy men
and women. They meet our pressing invitation, "All things are now
ready, come ye to the supper," with the reply, "Religion is meant to
prepare us for eternity, but we are far off from it as yet, and are still in
the hey-day of our being; there is plenty of time for those dreary
preparations for death. Your religion smells of the vault and the
worm. Let us be merry while we may. There will be room for more
serious considerations when we have enjoyed life a little, or have
become established in business, or can retire to live upon our savings.
Religion is for the sere and yellow leaf of the year's fall, when life
is fading, but not for the opening hours of spring, when the birds are
pairing and the primroses smiling upon the returning sun. You
prophesy of things that are for many days to come, and of times
that are far off." Very few young people may have *said* as much as
this, but that is the secret thought of many; and with this they resist
the admonition of the Holy Ghost, who saith, "To-day, if ye will hear
his voice, harden not your hearts." They put off the day of conversion,
as if it were a day of tempest and terror, and not, as it really is, a day
most calm, most bright, the bridal of the soul with heaven.

Let every unconverted person recollect that God knows what his
excuse is for turning a deaf ear to the voice of a dying Saviour's love.
You may not have spoken it to yourself so as to put it into words;
you might not even dare to do so, lest your conscience should be too
much startled: but God knows it all. He sees the hollowness, the
folly, and the wickedness of your excuses. He is not deceived by your
vain words, but makes short work with your apologies for delay.
Remember the parables of our Lord, and note that when the man of one
talent professed to think his master a hard man, he took him at his
word, and out of his own mouth condemned him; and in the case of
the invited guests who pleaded their farms and their merchandise as
excuses, no weight was attached to what they said, but the sentence
went forth, "None of these men that are bidden shall taste of my
supper." God knows the frivolity of your plea for delay, he knows
that you yourself are doubtful about it, and dare not stand to it so as
to give it anything like a solemn consideration. Very hard do you try
to deceive yourself into an easy state of conscience concerning it, but
in your inmost soul you are ashamed of your own falsehoods. My
business at this time is, by the aid of the Holy Spirit, to deal with
your consciences, and to convince you yet more thoroughly that delay
is unjustifiable, for the gospel has present demands upon you, and you
must not say, "The vision that he seeth is for many days to come, and
he prophesieth of the times that are far off."

I. For, first, *granted for a moment that the message we bring to you
has most to do with the future state, yet even then the day is not far off,
neither is there so great a distance between now and then, that you can
afford to wait.* Suppose that you are spared for threescore years and
ten. Young man, suppose that God spares you in your sins till the
snows of many winters shall whiten your head; young woman, suppose
that your now youthful countenance shall still escape the grave until
wrinkles are upon your brow; yet, still, how short will your life be!
You, perhaps, think seventy years a long period, but those who are

seventy, in looking back, will tell you that their age is an hand's breadth. I, who am but forty, feel at this time that every year flies more swiftly than the last ; and months and weeks are contracted into twinklings of the eye. The older one grows, the shorter one's life appears. I do not wonder that Jacob said, "Few and evil have the days of the years of my life been," for he spake as an extremely old man. Man is short-lived compared with his surroundings, he comes into the world and goes out of it, as a meteor flashes through yonder skies which have remained the same for ages. Listen to the brook which murmurs as it flows, and the meditative ear will hear it warble,

> " Men may come and men may go,
> But I go on for ever."

Look at yonder venerable oak, which has for five hundred years battled with the winds, and what an infant one seems when reclining beneath its shade ! Stand by some giant rock, which has confronted the tempests of the ages, and you feel like the insect of an hour. There are persons here to-night of seventy years of age who look back to the days of their boyhood as if they were but yesterday. Ask them, and they will tell you that their life seems to have been little more than a wink of the eye ; it has gone like a dream, or a lightning's flash—

> " What is life ? 'tis but a vapour,
> Soon it vanishes away."

Therefore do not say, "These things are for a far-off time;" for even if we could guarantee to you the whole length of human existence, it is but a span.

But there comes upon the heels of this a reflection never to be for-gotten—that not one man among us can promise himself, with any-thing like certainty, that he shall ever see threescore years and ten. We may survive, and by reason of strength we may creep up to four-score years ; yet not one of us can be sure that he shall do so ; the most of us will assuredly be gone long before that age. Nay, more, we cannot promise that we shall see half that length of time. You young men and women cannot be certain that you shall reach middle life. Let me check myself ! What am I talking of ? You cannot be certain that you will see this year out, and hear the bells ring in a new year. Yea, close upon you as to-morrow is, boast not yourselves of it, for it may never come ; or, should it come, you know not what it may bring forth to you, perhaps a coffin or a shroud. Ay, and this very night, when you close your eyes and rest your head upon your pillow, reckon not too surely that you shall ever again look on that familiar chamber, or go forth from it to the pursuits of life. It is clear, then, that the things which make for your peace are not matters for a far-off time, the frailty of life makes them necessities of this very hour. You are not far from your grave, you are nearer to it than when this discourse began : some of you are far nearer than you think.

To some this reflection comes with remarkable emphasis, for your occupation has enough of danger about it every day to furnish death with a hundred roads to convey you to his prison-house in the sepulchre. Can you look through a newspaper without meeting with the words "fatal accident," or "sudden death"? Travelling has many dangers, and even to cross the street is perilous. Men die at home, and when engaged about their lawful callings many are met by death. How true is this of those who go down to the sea in ships, or descend into the bowels of the earth in mines! But, indeed, no occupations are secure from death; a needle can kill as well as a sword; a scald, a burn, a fall, may end our lives, quite as readily as a pestilence or a battle. Does your business lead you to climb a ladder, it is no very perilous matter, but have you never heard of one who missed his footing and fell, never to rise again? You work amidst the materials of a rising building: have you never heard of stones that have fallen and have crushed the workers?

> ·· Dangers stand thick through all the ground
> To push us to the tomb,
> And fierce diseases wait around
> To hurry mortals home."

Notwithstanding all that can be done by sanitary laws, fevers are not unknown, and deadly strokes which fell men to the ground in an instant, as a butcher slays an ox, are not uncommon. Death has already removed many of your former companions. You have ridden into the battle of life, like the soldiers in the charge at Balaclava; and, young as you are in this warfare, you have seen saddles emptied right and left around you; you survive, but death has grazed you. The arrow of destruction has gone whizzing by your ear to find another mark; have you never wondered that it spared you? Amongst this congregation there are persons of delicate constitution. It grieves me to see so many fair daughters of our land with the mark of consumption upon their cheeks. Full well I know that lurid flame upon the countenance, and that strange lustre of the eye—signs of exhausting fires feeding upon life and consuming it too soon. Young men and women, many of you from the condition of your bodily frames can only struggle on till middle life, and scarcely that; for beyond thirty or forty you cannot survive. I fear that some of you have even in walking to this place felt a suspicious weariness, which argues exhaustion and decline. How can *you* say, when we talk to *you* about preparing to die, that we are talking about things that are far off? Dear souls, do not be so foolish. I implore you let these warnings lead you to decision. Far be it from me to cause you needless alarm, but is it needless? I am sure I love you too well to distress you without cause, but is there not cause enough? Come now, I press you most affectionately, answer me and say, does not your own reason tell you that my anxiety for you is not misplaced? Ought you not at once to lay to heart your Redeemer's call, and obey your Saviour's appeal? The time is short, catch the moments as they fly and hasten to be blest.

Remember also, once again, that even if you knew that you should escape from accident and fever and sudden death, yet there is one grand event that we too often forget, which may put an end to your day of mercy on a sudden. Have you never heard that Jesus Christ of Nazareth who was crucified on Calvary, died on the cross, and was laid in the tomb? Do you not know that he rose again the third day, and that after he had spent a little while with his disciples, he took them to the top of the Mount of Olives, and there before their eyes ascended into heaven, a cloud hiding him from their view? Have you forgotten the words of the angels, who said, "This same Jesus who is taken up from you into heaven shall so come in like manner as ye have seen him go into heaven"? Jesus will certainly come a second time to judge the world. Of that day and of that hour knoweth no man—no, not the angels of God. He will come as a thief in the night to an ungodly world; they shall be eating and drinking, and marrying and giving in marriage, just as they were when Noah entered into the ark, and they knew not until the flood came and swept them all away. In a moment—we cannot tell when, perhaps it may be ere next the words escape my lips—a sound far louder than any mortal voice will be heard above the clamours of worldly traffic, ay, and above the roaring of the sea. That sound as of a trumpet will proclaim the day of the Son of Man. "Behold, the Bridegroom cometh: go ye out to meet him," will sound throughout the church; and to the world there will ring out this clarion note, "Behold, he cometh with clouds, and every eye shall see him, and they also which crucified him." Jesus may come to-night. If he were to do so, would you then tell me that I am talking of far-off things? Did not Jesus say, "Behold, I come quickly!" and has not his church been saying, "Even so, come Lord Jesus"? His tarrying may be long to us, but to God it will be brief. We are to stand hourly watching and daily waiting for the coming of the Lord from heaven. Oh, I pray you do not say that the Lord delayeth his coming, for that was the language of the wicked servant who was cut in pieces, and it is the mark of the mockers of the last days, that they say, "Where is the promise of his coming?" Be ye not mockers, lest your bands be made strong; but listen to the undoubted voice of prophecy and of the word of God, "Behold, I come quickly." "Be ye also ready, for in such an hour as ye think not the Son of Man cometh."

Now, then, it is clear enough that even if the gospel message did concern only our life in another world, yet still it is unwise for men to say, "The vision is for many days to come, and he prophesieth of the times that are far off."

II. But, secondly, I have to remind you that *our message really deals with the present.* The blessings of the gospel have as much to do with this present life as with existence beyond the tomb.

For observe, first, we are sent to plead with you, young men and women, and tenderly to remind you that you are at this hour acting unjustly and unkindly towards your God. He made you, and you do not serve him; he has kept you alive, and you are not obedient to him. He has sent the word of his gospel to you, and you have not received it; he has sent his only begotten Son, and you have despised him. This injustice is a thing of the present; and the appeal we make to you about it is, that in all reason such conduct should come to an end. Oh, may God's Holy Spirit help you to end it! If I feel that I have done any man an injustice, I am eager to set it right, I would not wait till to-morrow, I wish to make him amends at once. Yes, and even when I have forgotten to render assistance to some needy widow, I

chide myself, and feel uneasy till I have attended to the matter. Do
you not feel the same? Would you wilfully wrong or neglect another?
I feel sure you would not. How is it, then, that you can be content
to be unjust to God, cruel to the dear Lover of the souls of men, and
antagonistic to the loving pleadings of the Holy Spirit? That first
chapter of Isaiah—you remember it, how striking it is! Why, if men
had hearts that were at all tender it would break them. Read it.
" Hear, O heavens, and give ear, O earth. I have nourished and
brought up children, and they have rebelled against me. The ox
knoweth his owner, and the ass his master's crib; but Israel doth not
know; my people doth not consider." It is the wail of God himself
over man's unkindness to his Maker! Young man of honour, young
man of integrity, does nothing speak to your conscience in this?
" Will a man rob God?" You would not rob your employer. You
would not like to be thought unfaithful or dishonest towards man; and
yet your God, your God, your God—is he to be treated so basely, notwithstanding all his goodness? As Jesus said, " For which of these
works do you stone me?" so does Jehovah say, " I have made you; I
have kept the breath in your nostrils; I have fed you all your life
long; and for which of all these good things do you live without me,
and neglect me, and perhaps even curse my name, and sin with a high
hand against my sacred law?" Now, can you think it right to
remain in so wantonly unjust a course of life as this? Can it be right
to continue to wrong your God and grieve his matchless love? Pro-
voke him no more, I pray you. Let conscience lead you to feel that
you have dealt ill with the Lord, and come ye to him for forgiveness
and change of heart. O Spirit of God, make this appeal to be felt by
these beloved youths and maidens!

Again, our message has to do with the present, for we would affectionately remind you that you are now at enmity with your best
friend—the friend to whose love you owe everything. You have
grieved him, and are, without cause, his enemy; can you bear this
thought? I know a little child who had done something wrong,
and her kind father talked to her, and at last, as a punishment,
he said to her in a very sad voice, " I cannot kiss you to-night,
for you have grieved me very much." That broke her little heart.
Though not a stroke had been laid upon her, she saw sorrow in
her dear father's face, and she could not endure it. She pleaded
and wept and pleaded again to be forgiven. It was thought wise
to withhold the kiss, and she was sent to bed, for she had done
very wrong; but there was no sleep for those weeping eyes, and
when mother went up to that little one's chamber she heard frequent
sobs and sighs, and a sorrowful little voice said, " I was very, very
naughty, but pray forgive me, and ask dear father to give me a
kiss." She loved her father, and she could not bear that he should
be grieved. Child of mercy, erring child of the great Father of
spirits, canst thou bear to live for ever at enmity with the loving
Father? " Would he forgive me?" say you. What makes you ask
the question? Is it that you do not know how good he is? Has he
not pourtrayed himself as meeting his prodigal son and falling upon
his neck and kissing him? Before the child had reached the father,

the father had reached the child. The father was eager to forgive, and therefore, when the son was yet a great way off his father saw him, and ran, and had compassion. Say no longer that we are talking of things of a far-off time? It is not so. I am speaking of that which I pray may be true to you to-night, that you may not remain enemies to God even another hour, but now may become his dear repenting children, and fly into your tender Father's arms.

I have to remind you, however, of much more than this, namely, that you are this night in danger. On account of your treatment of God, and your remaining an enemy to him, he will surely visit you in justice and punish you for your transgressions. He is a just God, and every sin committed is noted in his book; and there it stands recorded against his judgment day. The danger you are in is that you may this moment go down into the pit; and while sitting in that pew may bow your head in death and appear before your Maker in an instant, to receive the just reward of your sins. We come to tell you that there is immediate pardon for all the sins of those who will believe in the Lord Jesus Christ, and that if you will believe in Jesus, your sins, which are many, are all forgiven you. Know ye not the story (ye have heard it many a time) that the Lord Jesus took upon himself the sins of all who trust him, and suffered, in their room and stead, the penalty due to their sins? He was our substitute, and as such he died, the just for the unjust, to bring us to God. He laid down his life for us, that " whosoever believeth in him should not perish, but have everlasting life." Will you refuse the salvation so dearly purchased but so freely presented? Will you not accept it here, and now? Can you bear the burden of your sins? Are you content to abide for a single hour in peril of eternal punishment? Can you bear to be slipping down into the open jaws of hell as you now are? Remember God's patience will not last for ever; long enough have you provoked him. All things are weary of you. The very earth on which you stand groans beneath the indignity of bearing a sinner upon its surface. So long as you are an enemy to God, the stones of the field are against you, and all creation threatens you. It is a wonder that you do not sink at once to destruction. For this cause we would have you pardoned *now* and made free from divine wrath *now*. The peril is immediate, the Lord grant that so the rescue may be. Do I hear you say, " But may pardon be had at once? Is Jesus Christ a present Saviour? We thought that we might perhaps find him when we came to die, or might obtain a hope of mercy after living a long life of seeking." It is not so. Free grace proclaims immediate salvation from sin and misery. Whosoever looks to Jesus at this very moment shall have his sins forgiven. At the instant he believes in the Lord Jesus, the sinner shall cease to be in danger of the fires of hell. The moment a man turns his eye of faith to Jesus Christ he is saved from the wrath to come. It is present salvation that we preach to you, and the present comfort of that present salvation, too.

Many other reasons tend to make this weighty matter exceedingly pressing; and among them is this, that there is a disease in your heart, the disease of sin, and it needs immediate cure. I do not hear persons say, if they discover an incipient disease in their systems, that they will wait a while till the evil is more fully developed, and will then resort to a physician. The most of us have sense enough to try to check disease at once. Young man, thou hast a leprosy upon thee. Young woman, thou hast a dreadful malady within thy heart. Dost thou not desire to be healed now? Jesus can give thee immediate healing if thou believest in him. Wilt thou hesitate to be made whole? Dost thou love thy mortal malady? Is hideous sin so dear to thee? O that thou wouldst cry to be saved immediately, then will Jesus hear thee. His Spirit will descend upon thee, and cleanse thee, give thee a new heart, and a right spirit, yea, and make thee whole from this time henceforth and for ever; canst thou wish to have so great a blessing postponed? Surely a sick man can never be cured too soon.

The gospel which we preach to you will also bring you present blessings. In addition to present pardon and present justification, it will give you present regeneration, present adoption, present sanctification, present access to God, present peace through believing, and present help in time of trouble, and it will make you even for this life doubly happy. It will be wisdom for your way, strength for your conflict, and comfort for your sorrow. If I had to die like a dog I would still wish to be a Christian. If there were no hereafter—though the supposition is not to be tolerated—yet still let me live for and with Jesus, my beloved Lord. Balaam chose the righteous man's death, I choose it too, but quite as much do I choose his life, for to have the love of God in the heart, to have peace with God, to be able to look up to heaven with confidence, and talk to my heavenly Father in childlike trustfulness is a present joy and comfort worth more than worlds. Young men and women, in preaching to you the gospel, we are preaching that which is good for this life as well as for the life to come. If you believe in Jesus you will be saved now, on the spot, and you will now enjoy the unchanging favour of God, so that you will go your way henceforth not to live as others do, but as the chosen of God, beloved with special love, enriched with special blessings, to rejoice every day till you are taken up to dwell where Jesus is. Present salvation is the burden of the Lord's message to you, and therefore it is not true, but infamously false, that the vision is for many days to come, and the prophecy for times that are far off. Is there not reason in my pleadings? If so, yield to them. Can you answer these arguments? If not, I pray you cease delaying. Again would I implore the Holy Spirit to lead you to immediate decision.

III. My third point is, that *I shall not deny, but I shall glory rather in admitting, that the gospel has to do with the future.* Albeit, that it is not exclusively a revelation for far-off times, yet it is filled with glorious hopes and bright prospects concerning things to come.

The gospel of Jesus Christ has to do with the whole of a young man's life. If you receive Jesus Christ you will not merely have him to-night, but that faith by which you receive him will operate upon your whole existence throughout time and eternity. Dear young friends, if you are saved while yet you are young you will find religion to be a great preventive of sin. What a blessing it is not to have been daubed with the slime of Sodom, never to have had our bones broken by actual vice. Many who have been saved from a life of crime will nevertheless be spiritual cripples for life ! To be snatched out of the vortex of vice is cause for great gratitude, but to have been kept out of it is better. It is doubly well, if the grace of God comes upon us while still we are untainted by the pollution of the world, and have not gone into excess of riot. Before dissolute habits have undermined the constitution, and self-indulgence has degraded the mind, it is above all things well to have the heart renewed. Prevention is better than cure, and grace gives both. Thank God that you are still young, and pray earnestly that you may now receive grace to cleanse your way by taking heed thereto, according to his word.

Grace will also act as a preservative as well as a preventive. The good thing which God will put in you will keep you. I bless God I have not to preach a temporary salvation to you at this time. That which charmed me about the gospel when I was a lad was its power to preserve from sinning. I saw some of my school companions who had been highly commended for their character, and were a little older than myself, become sad offenders when they left home. I used to hear sad stories of their evil actions when they had gone to London to be apprenticed, or to take positions in large establishments, and I reasoned thus with myself: " When I leave my father's house I shall be tempted, too, and I have the same heart that they have, indeed, I have not been even as good as they have been ; the probabilities are, therefore, that I shall plunge into sin as they have done." I felt horrified with that. I could not bear that I should cause my mother to shed tears over a dissolute son, or break my father's heart with debauchery. The thought could not be endured, and when I heard that whosoever believed in the Lord Jesus Christ should be saved, I understood that he would be saved from sinning, and I laid hold upon Jesus to preserve me from sin, and he has done it. I committed my character to Christ, and he has preserved me to this day, and I believe he will not let me go. I recommend to you, young men, a character-insurance, in the form of believing in Jesus Christ. Dear young woman, may that modest cheek of yours never need to blush for deed of shame ; may your delicate purity of feeling never be lost through gross defiling sin : but remember, it may be so unless the Lord keeps you : I commend to you the blessed preserving power of faith in Christ Jesus, which will secure for you the Holy Spirit to dwell in you and abide in you, and sanctify you all your days. I know I speak to some who shudder at the thought of vice. Trained as you have been by Christian parents, and under the holiest influences, you would rather die than act as some who disgrace their father's name ; I know you would. But you must not trust your own hearts ; you may yet become as bad as others or worse than they unless your natures are renewed, and only Jesus Christ can do that, by the power of the Holy Spirit. Whosoever believeth in him has passed from death unto life ; he shall not live in sin, but he shall be preserved in holiness even to the end.

My dear young friends, if God shall be pleased to change your hearts to-night, as I pray he may, you will be prepared for the future. You have not fully entered into the battle of life yet. You have your way to make, your professions and trades to choose. You, young

women, are still under the parental wing ; you have domestic relation-
ships yet to form. Now, consider how well prepared you will be for
life's work and service if you give your hearts to Jesus. Young man,
you will be the right man to enter a large establishment : with the
grace of God in your heart you will be a blessing there. Though
surrounded by her snares in this wicked city, the strange woman will
in vain hunt for your precious life ; and other vices will be unable to
pollute you. Young woman, you will have wisdom to choose for your
life's companion no mere fop and fool, but one who loves the Lord as
you will do, with whom you may hope to spend happy and holy days.
You will have placed within yourself resources of joy and pleasure
which will never fail ; there will be a well of living water within you
which will supply you with joy and comfort and consolation, even
amid trial and distress. You will be prepared for whatever is to come.
A young Christian is fit to be made an emperor or a servant, if God
shall call him to either post. If you want the best materials for a
model prince, or a model peasant, you shall find it in the child of
God ; only, mark you, the man who is a child of God is less likely to
sink into utter destitution, because he will be saved from the vices of
extravagance and idleness which are the frequent causes of poverty ;
and, probably, on the other hand, he is less likely to become a prince,
for seldom has God lifted his own children to places so perilous. You
will be ready, young man, for any future, if your heart be right with
God. And do you know when I think of you, and of what the Lord
may make of you, I feel an intense respect, as well as love, for you.
I hope none of us will be lacking in respect to old age, it is honourable,
and it is to be esteemed and reverenced ; but I feel frequently inclined
to do homage to your youth. When a celebrated tutor entered his
school-room, he always took off his hat to his boys, because as he
said he did not know which of them might yet turn out to be a
poet, a bishop, a lord chancellor, or a prime minister. When I look
at young men and women, I feel much the same, for I do not
know what they are to be. I may be addressing to-night a Living-
stone, or a Moffat. I may be speaking to-night to a John Howard,
or a Wilberforce : I may be addressing a Mrs. Judson, or an
Elizabeth Fry. I may be speaking to some whom God will kindle
into great lights to bless the sons of men for many a day, and
afterwards to shine as the stars for ever and ever. But you cannot
shine if you are not lighted. You cannot bless God and bless the sons
of men unless God first blesses you. Unregenerate, you are useless.
Born again, you will be born for usefulness, but while you are unconverted your usefulness is being lost. I will not insinuate that I
expect every one here to become famous. It is not even desirable ;
but I do know this, that every one whose heart shall be given to Jesus,
will be so useful and so necessary to the Church and to the world, that
this world without them would lack a benefactor, and heaven's company would be incomplete unless they joined its ranks. Oh, the value
of a redeemed soul ! The importance of a young life ! I wish I could
multliply myself into a thousand bodies that I might come round and
take the hand of every young person here, as he or she shall leave the
Tabernacle, and say, " By the preciousness of your life, by the hallowed

uses to which you may be put, by the good that you may do, and by
the glory you may bring to God, do not think of pardon and grace
as things of the future ; but now, even now, lay hold of them, and
they will become to you the great power by which you shall benefit
your generation and go down to the grave with honour."

When I grow grey, if God shall spare me—may I see around me
some of you with whom I speak to-day, who shall be some twenty
years younger than myself, of whom I shall say, " My former deacons
and elders are either very old or have gone home to heaven ; the
dear men of God who were with me when I was forty years of age
have passed away ; but those whom I preached to on that night in
March, 1874, have come to fill their places.   Those dear sisters who
used to conduct the classes, teach the school, and manage the various
societies for the poor, have gone, and we have followed them to their
graves and wept over them, but here come their daughters to fill their
places."   I pray that names honoured in our churches may never die
out from our midst ; may the fathers live again in their children.   It
may not be my honour to be succeeded in this pulpit by one of my
own sons, greatly as I would rejoice if it might be so, but at least
I hope they will be here in this church to serve their father's God,
and to be regarded with affection by you for the sake of him who
spent his life in your midst.   I pray that all my honoured brethren
may have sons and daughters in the church—ay, from generation to
generation may there be those in our assemblies—of whom it shall
be said, "These are of the old stock : they keep up the old name."
I wish this felicity to all the churches, that instead of the fathers
may be the children whom thou mayest make princes in all the
earth.   Brethren of my own age, we shall soon die : God grant us to
die at our posts.   The standard-bearer will fall, and in his last embrace
he will press the standard to his heart, for it is dearer than life to him.
But courage, my brethren, our sons will urge on the sacred war, and carry
on the good old cause to victory.   What say ye, dear ones ?   Do not
your hearts say "Amen"?   Young men, will you not take up the blood-
stained banner when we shall go our ways ?   Sons and daughters of
the faithful, will you desert your fathers' God ?   Oh, will it be that he
whom we love shall be despised by you?   Will you turn your back on
the Christ who was all in all to us ?   No.   It cannot be.   Be of good
cheer, Abraham, Isaac shall succeed thee, Jacob shall rise up to
serve thy God, Jacob shall live to see his son Joseph, and even to bless
Ephraim and Manasseh ; and so from generation to generation shall
the Lord be praised.

Thus far concerning this life, but now let me remind you, dear young
friends, that if your hearts be given to Christ you need not tremble
about the end of life.   You may look forward to it with hope.   It
will come.   Thank God, it will come !   Have you never wished that
you could ride to heaven in a chariot of fire, like Elijah ?   I did once
till I reflected that if a chariot of fire should come for me I should
be more afraid to get into it than to lie down and die upon my bed ;
and of the two one might prefer to die, for to die in the Lord is to be
made like to our glorious Head.   I see no joy in the hope of escaping
death.   Jesus died, and so let me die.   On his dear face the seal of

death was set, so let it be on mine, that I may talk of resurrection as they cannot who shall be changed at his coming. You need not be afraid to depart and be with Christ, which is far better. Young people, whether you die in youth or old age, if you are resting in Jesus you shall sit upon the banks of Jordan singing. As our friends sang last night :—

"Never mind the river."

The parting song will be sweet, but oh, the glory! Oh, the glory! I will not try to paint it. Who can? The judgment will come, but you will not tremble at it. On the right hand shall you stand, for who can condemn those for whom Christ has died? The conflagration of the globe will come, the elements shall melt with fervent heat; but you will not tremble, for you shall be caught up together with the Lord in the air, and so shall you be for ever with the Lord. Hell shall swallow up the unjust, they shall go down alive into the pit; but you shall not tremble for that, for you are redeemed by the precious blood. The millennial glory, whatever that may be; and the reign with Christ, and the triumph over death and hell; and the giving up of the kingdom to God, even the Father, when God shall be all in all; and eternity with all its infinite glory; these shall be all yours. If you had to go through hell to reach this glory, it would be worth the cost! But you have not to do any such thing; you have only to believe in Jesus, and even faith is the Lord's own gracious gift. " Look unto me and be ye saved, all ye ends of the earth." This is the gospel. Look! Look! Look! 'Tis but a look. Look, blear-eyed soul, thou who canst scarce see for ignorance! Look, thou whose eyes are swimming in tears! Look, thou who seest hell before thee! Look, thou who art sinking into the jaws of perdition! Look ye ends of the earth, that are farthest gone in sin, if such be here! Ye who are plunged deep in iniquity— look! 'Tis Jesus on the cross ye are bidden to look at—yea, Jesus at the right hand of God, the crucified Son of Man exalted at the right hand of the Father. Look unto him, and be ye saved, for he is God, and beside him there is none else.

God grant to you to look to Jesus, even now, for his name's sake. Amen.

4 The Best Burden for Young Shoulders

"It is good for a man that he bear the yoke in his youth."—Lamentations iii. 27.

YOKE-BEARING is not pleasant, but it is good. It is not every pleasant thing that is good, nor every good thing that is pleasant. Sometimes the goodness may be just in proportion to the unpleasantness. Now, it is childish to be always craving for sweets; those who by reason of use have had their senses exercised, should prefer the wholesome to the palatable. It ought to reconcile us to that which is unsavoury when we are informed that it is good! A little child is not easily reconciled that way, because, as yet, he cannot think and judge; but the man of God ought to find it very easy to quiet every murmur and complaint as soon as he perceives that, though unpleasant, the thing is good. Since, my dear friends, we are not very good judges ourselves of that which is good for us, any more than our children are, and since we expect our little ones to leave the choice of their diet with us, will it not be wise of us to leave everything with our heavenly Father? We can judge what is pleasant, but we cannot discern that which is good for us, but HE can judge, and therefore it will be always well for us to leave all our affairs in his hands, and say, "Nevertheless, not as I will, but as thou wilt." Since we are quite certain upon Scriptural authority that whatever the Lord sends to his people will work out their benefit, we ought to be perfectly resigned to the Lord's will; nay, much more, we ought to be thankful for all his appointments even when they displease the flesh, being quite certain that his will is the best that can be, and that if we could see the end from the beginning it is exactly what we should choose, if we were as wise and good as our heavenly Father is. Our shoulders bow themselves with gladness to the burden which Jesus declares to be profitable unto us: this assurance from his lips makes his yoke easy to bear.

Our text tells us of something which, though not very comfortable, is good.—"It is good for a man that he bear the yoke in his youth." The

No. 1,291.

illustration is drawn from cattle. The bullocks have to bear the yoke. They go in pairs, and the yoke is borne upon their shoulders. The yoke is somewhat burdensome. If the bullock is not broken-in when it is young it will never make a good ploughing ox. It will be fretted and troubled with the labour it will have to do; it will be very hard work to drive it, and the husbandman will accomplish but little ploughing. It is good for the bullock to be brought into subjection while it is young, and so it is with all sorts of animals: the horse must be broken-in while he is a colt; and if a certain period of that horse's life be allowed to pass over without its being under the trainer's hand, it will never make a thoroughly useful horse. If you want to train a dog you must take him while he is young, and teach him his work. That is the metaphor. It is just so with men. It is good for us that we be broken-in while we are yet young, and learn to bear the yoke in our youth.

If you take the text naturally as uttering a truth of ordinary life, it is still worth considering. Even apart from the grace of God, and apart from religion, it is a great blessing for a man to bear the yoke in his youth! that is to say, first, *it is good for us when we are young to learn obedience.* It is half the making of a man to be placed under rule, and taught to bear restraint. When young people grow older they will have to be very much a law unto themselves, there may be no father living to warn them lovingly, and no mother to guide them gently; young people will be older people, and govern themselves, and no one is fit to do that till he has learned to be obedient. The proverb is, "Boys will be boys," but I do not think so,—they will be men if we let them have time, and unless they learn self-restraint and habits of obedience while they are boys, they are not likely to make good men. He who cannot obey is not fit to rule: he who never learned to submit will make a tyrant when he obtains the power. It is good that every child should be broken in, delivered from his foolish self-will, and made to feel that he has superiors, masters, and governors, and, then, when it shall come to his turn to be a leader and a master he will have the more kindly fellow-feeling to those who are under him. Be you sure of this, that if he does not learn the drill of obedience he will never be a good soldier in the battle of life.

It is good for young people to bear the yoke, too, in the sense of giving themselves in their early days to acquire knowledge. If we do not learn when we are young, when shall we learn? Some who have begun to study late in life, have yet achieved a good deal, but it has been with much difficulty. If you do not use the machinery of the mind in youth, it gets rusty; but if it is used from the very first, and kept continually in action and well oiled, it will go on easily throughout the whole of life. Our early days are favourable to the acquirement of knowledge, and every lad that is an apprentice should make the best of his apprentice-ship: he will never make much of a journeyman if he does not. Every man that is starting in life, while he is yet young should do all that he possibly can to acquire a full equipment, for if he does not he will know the miss of it sooner or later. If a man starts upon life's voyage and has left his anchor at home, or forgotten his stores, he will find out his deficiencies when he gets to sea; and when the storm begins to howl through the cordage he will wish that he had listened to the dictates of prudence, and had been better prepared for life's perilous voyage.

It is good for young people, too—we are now talking about the natural meaning of the passage—*good for them that they should encounter difficulties and troubles when they begin life.* The silver spoon in the mouth with which some people are born is very apt to choke them. There are hundreds of people who have never been able to speak out because of that dreadful silver spoon. It is not every man that is the richer in the long run, even in mere gold and silver, for having commenced with capital. I believe you will generally find that the rich men who have been "self-made," as they call it, came to London with a half-crown in their pockets; I have noticed that thirty pence is about the amount they leave home with; and that half-crown, neither less nor more, becomes the nest egg of a fortune. Young men who begin with thousands of pounds often end with nothing at all. It is good for a man that he should have a rough battle when life begins, that he should not be lapped in dainty ease, and find everything arranged according to his will : he will never develop his muscle, he will never make a man, unless there is hard work for him to do. Those long hours, that stern thinking, those weary bones, and all that, of which young people now-a-days are very apt to complain, though they do not work half as hard as their fathers, nor above a tenth as hard as their grandfathers—all these things within reason and measure help to make men, and I only hope that the easier times, which are now happily in fashion, may not breed a softer and a less manly nature among our young men. It is good for a man that he should bear the yoke of labour, trial, and difficulty in his youth, and if we could lift the yoke from every weary shoulder it would not be wise to do so. Many a man who has succeeded in life is very thankful to God that he had in his early years to bear a little poverty, and to work hard and toil, for he never would have come to be what he is if it had not been for the strengthening and educating influence of trial.

It is not, however, my business to preach about these matters at any length; I am not a moral lecturer, but a minister of the gospel. I have fulfilled a duty when I have given the first meaning to the text, and now I shall use it for nobler ends.

I. First of all, IT IS GOOD TO BE A CHRISTIAN WHILE YOU ARE YOUNG. It is good for a man to bear Christ's yoke in his youth.

I shall not ask you to pardon me if I here speak as one who has tried and proved it. Surely I may do so without egotism, for it is not mine own honour, but God's, that I shall speak of. What the Lord has wrought in me, of that I will speak. At fifteen years of age I was brought to know the Lord, and to confess him, and I can therefore speak as one who bore the yoke in his youth; and, young people, if I have never to address you again, I should like to say to you, it has been good for me. Ah, how good I cannot tell you, but so good that I earnestly wish that every one of you would bear my Master's yoke in his youth : I could not wish you a greater blessing.

For, see, first, the man whose heart is conquered by divine grace early *is made happy soon.* That is a blessed prayer in the psalm, " O satisfy us *early* with thy mercy, that we may rejoice and be glad all our days."

Very few people, if they understood it, would wish to postpone happiness. Young hearts generally ask to be happy *now*. To have sin forgiven is to be unloaded *now* of that which is the prime cause o. sorrow. To receive the righteousness of Jesus Christ by faith is to be clothed with peace now. To be reconciled to God is to have a spring of consolation within your soul *now*. To know yourself to be God's child is to have the greatest joy out of heaven, and to have it *now*. Who would wish to postpone it? Young Christians may die, but it is of small conse-quence if they do, for being early in Christ, they will be early in heaven. Who would not wish to be safe as soon as possible? Who desires to tarry in the land of peril, where a point of time, a moment's space, may shut you up in hell? To be early secured from the wrath to come— early endued with a sense of security in Jesus Christ—why surely it does not want many words to prove that this is good!

Besides, while early piety brings early happiness, let it never be for-gotten that *it s ives from a thousand snares*. There are things which a man knows, who has lived long in sin, which he wishes he could forget! God's grace rinses your mouth after you have been eating the forbidden fruit, but the flavour is very apt to linger, and to return. Songs which are libels upon God and upon decency, once heard, will attack you in the middle of a prayer; and words which, if you could forget them, you might be willing to lose your memory for that purpose, will invade your most hallowed seasons. It is a great mercy that if a man be seventy or eighty years of age, yet if he shall believe in the Lord Jesus Christ, he shall be saved! Eleventh hour mercies are very sweet. But what a double privilege it is to be set to work in the vineyard while yet the dew is on the leaves, and so to be kept from the idleness and the wickedness of the market place in which others loiter so long.

It is good for a man to bear Christ's yoke in his youth because *it saves him from having those shoulders galled with the devil's yoke*. It preserves him from the fetters of that pitiful slavery into which so many are brought by habits long acquired and deeply seated. Sins long indulged grow to the shoulders, and to remove them is like tearing away one's flesh. Be thankful, young people, that the Saviour is ready to receive you while you are yet young, and that he gives you the promise, "They that seek me early shall find me." Happy they who entertain the Redeemer in the morning, and so shut out the evil spirit all day long.

There is this goodness about it, again, that *it gives you longer time in which to serve God*. If I were taken into the service of one whom I loved, I should like to do him a long day's work. If I knew that I could only work for him one day, I should strive to begin as soon as the grey light of dawn permitted me to see, and I would continue at work far into the evening, cheerfully active, so long as a glimmer re-mained. If you are converted late in life you can only give to our Lord Jesus the shades of evening. Blessed be his name, he will accept eventide service; but still, how much better to be able to serve the Lord from your youth up, to give him those bright days while the birds are singing in the soul, when the sun is unclouded, and the shadows are not falling; and then to give him the long evening, when at eventide he makes it light, and causes the infirmities of age to display his power and his fidelity. I think I know of no grander sight

than that of a grey-haired man who has served the Lord Jesus from
his youth up.

There is this goodness about it yet further, that *it enables one to be
well established in divine things.* "They that are planted in the courts
of the Lord shall flourish in the courts of our God." A tree trans-
planted takes a certain time to root, but when it becomes well established
it produces abundant fruit. There must be time for striking root in divine
things; everything in the kingdom of grace is not to be learned in ten
minutes. I bless God that a man who has believed in Jesus only one
second is a saved man; but he is not an instructed man, he is not
an established man. He is not trained for battle; nor tutored for
labour. These things take time. When we are converted we go to
school to Christ, we sit at his feet and learn of him. Now, who is the
best scholar? All other things being equal, I should expect to find
the best scholars in the school to be those who come early. Eleven
o'clock scholars do not learn much; evening scholars, with a good master
and great diligence, may pick up something, but scarcely so much as
those who have been at the school all day. Oh, how blessed it is to
begin to know Christ very early, because then you can go on compre-
hending with all saints the heights and depths of that which surpasseth
knowledge. No fear that you will ever exhaust this knowledge; it is so
infinitely great and blessed, that if we lived seven thousand years in the
world, there would still be more to know of Christ, and we should still
have to say, "Oh, the depths." We need not be afraid, therefore, that
if we are converted when we are ten, or fifteen, or twenty years of age,
we shall live to wear out the freshness of religion. Ah, no, we shall
love it more and understand it better, and by God's grace practice it
more fully as the years roll over us. Hence it is so good to begin soon.

And then, let me say, *it gives such confidence in after life to have
given your heart to Jesus young.*

I am glad to see some boys and girls here to-night. Now, my dear
children, God may spare you to become old men and old women, and
when your hair is grey and you are getting feeble, and you know that
you will soon die, it will be very delightful to be able to say, "O Lord,
I have known thee from my youth, and hitherto have I declared thy
wondrous works. Now also when I am old and grey-headed, O God,
forsake me not." There will be much force in the plea, for if we have
a faithful servant, we do not cast him off when he grows old. "Ah,"
you say, "he cannot do much now. The old man is getting very
feeble, he cannot see or hear as he used to do, and he is slow in his
movements: but, then, you see, the good old fellow has been in our
family ever since he was a boy, and you do not think we are going
to turn him off now?" No, the Lord will not cast off his old
servants. He will not say to them "I have had the best of you; I have
had your young days, and I have had your middle life, but now you
may go begging, and take care of yourself." No, that is how the Amale-
kite or the Ishmaelite might talk, but the God of Israel never forsakes
his people. He says, "Even to your old age I am he; and even to
hoar hairs will I carry you; I have made; and I will bear; even I will
carry, and will deliver you." O, you who have given yourselves to
Jesus through his rich and sovereign grace while you are young, I know

you feel it a sweet plea to urge with God—"Now, Lord, forsake me not." So, then, young people, if you would lay by a precious treasure of consolation when those that look out of the windows are darkened, if you would have strength for the time of weakness, if you would have comfort for the day when the mourners go about the streets, if, above all, you would be supported when you are going to your long home, yield yourselves to Jesus now. Oh, that this very night you may bow your shoulders to the easy yoke of the meek and lowly Saviour ; so shall you find rest unto your souls.

II. I shall now give another meaning to the text ; may the Holy Spirit bless it. Secondly, IT IS GOOD FOR YOUNG CHRISTIANS THAT THEY BEAR THE YOKE OF JESUS. What do we mean by that?

A good number of you have been lately converted, and to you I speak most earnestly. It will be for your good as long as ever you live to render to Jesus *complete obedience at the very first*. Some Christians seem to me to start to Canaan all in a muddle ; they do not begin their pilgrimage in the right pilgrim fashion. Every young Christian when he is converted should take time to consider, and should say to himself, " What am I to do ? What is the duty of a Christian ? " He should also devoutly say to the Lord Jesus, " Lord, show me what thou wouldst have me to do," and wait upon the Holy Ghost for guidance.

Two young lads were not long ago converted to God ; one of them attended here, the other at another place of worship. They talked to each other about what was the right way of confessing Jesus Christ: they did not quite know, but they meant to find out. They borrowed the keys of a neighbouring Independent chapel, and went inside and spent some hours day after day reading together the New Testament, and turning to every passage which refers to baptism. The result was that they both of them came and were baptized in this place. I wish that all Christians in commencing would look at that ordinance, and at every other point in dispute, and see what is God's mind about it. Search the Scriptures and see for yourselves. Do not say, " I have always been with the Episcopalians, and therefore I ought to do as they do at church." Or " I have always been with the Baptists," or "with the Wesleyans." My dear friends, these people cannot make rules for us. Here is our guide—this Bible. If I want to go by the railway, I use Bradshaw, and do not trust to hearsay ; and if I want to go to heaven I must follow the Bible. There is another book which people will ask you to attend to. Well, we will say nothing against that book, only it is not *the* book. *The* book is this volume, the blessed Bible. You should begin by feeling, " My Lord has saved me ; I am his servant, and I mean at once to take his yoke upon me. I will, as far as ever I can, do what he would have me do. There are some sins into which I shall most likely fall. Watch as I may, I shall sometimes make a slip, but here are some things which I can be right about, and I will take care that I am right about them." Now, if you young people begin conscientiously studying the word, and desiring in everything to put your feet down where Christ put his feet, I am sure it will be good for you. You will grow up to be healthy Christians, and men of no ordinary stature. But if you do not begin with searching the word, but take your religion at second-hand from other people, and do what you see other people do, without searching, why, you will lack that noble independence of mind and courage of spirit, and, at the same time, that complete submission to Christ, which make up the main elements of a noble-minded Christian.

It is good for a man that he bear the yoke in his youth, in the next place, namely, by *attaining clear instruction in divine truth.* We ought to go to the Lord Jesus Christ to learn of him, not merely about ordinances and actions, but about what to think and what to believe. Oh, how I wish that every one of us had begun, with regard to our doctrinal sentiments, by presenting our minds to Christ like a sheet of clear paper for his Holy Spirit to write the truth thereon. Alas, we begin with many a line upon us written by the pen of prejudice. Dear friend, if you are converted to God, you are now to sit at the feet of Jesus, to learn everything from him—not to take your views to him. Those are common expressions, " my views," and " my opinions," and "I am of such a persuasion." Beloved, be persuaded by Christ, for that is the only persuasion worth following. Take your *views* from him : no other views of eternal and heavenly things are worth having. " Oh," says one, " but then they might not happen to be *your* views." Just so, and I do not ask you to take my views ; on the other hand I charge you before God never to believe anything because I say it, but to hearken only to my Master, and yield your faith only to the infallible book. We urge this upon you because, even if you believe the truth because we say it, you have not believed it in the right way. Truth is to be received because it is *true*, and because Jesus Christ's authority proves it *to you* to be true, not because any poor mortal who happens to preach is supposed to possess authority to decide such questions. We have no authority to assert anything to be truth upon our own *ipse dixit*. We are simply the trumpets at the lips of Christ when we speak with power ; and sometimes, alas, we blow our own trumpets instead of leaving Jesus Christ to blow through us, and then we are worse than useless. I charge you bear the yoke in your youth by studying hard to know what is the way, and the truth, and the life, from the lips of Jesus Christ himself, being taught of the Spirit of God. It is good for you to do this.

It is good for young converts also to bear the yoke by beginning to serve Jesus Christ early. I like to see the mother when she brings her little one to the house of God put the penny into its hand, and teach it early to contribute to the cause of Christ; and when people are converted there is nothing like their having something to do very soon. Not that they are to attempt to do the major things which belong to the more advanced and instructed ; for, concerning some of these, we should apply the rule, " Not a novice, lest being lifted up with pride, he fall into the condemnation of the devil." But there is work for every believer to do in Christ's vineyard. There is work for children, there is work for young men, work for young women, and it is good to begin early. The Lord Jesus Christ, who was so pleased with the widow's mite, is very pleased with a child's love to him. We big people are very apt to think, " What can a little girl do for Jesus ?" Oh, but if that little girl does not do something for Jesus now that she is saved, she will very likely grow up to be an idle Christian, and not serve God in after years as she should.

I like to see the little trees which they put into our gardens, you know, the little pyramids, and other dwarf trees ; I like to see them even from the first bear just a little fruit. I think, sometimes, that pears, when there are only one or two on the tree, are far finer in flavour than those on the big tree, which too often have lost in quality what they have gained in quantity. That which is done for Jesus Christ by young Christians, by weak Christians, by timid Christians, often has a very delicate flavour about it, precious to the taste of Jesus. It is good to begin serving him in our youth.

"Ah," says one, "I shall begin when I can preach." Will you? You had better begin writing a letter to that young friend with whom you went to school. You had better begin by dropping a tract down an area, or by trying to speak to some young person of your own age. Pride will prompt you to wish to be great, but love to Jesus will teach you that the small things are acceptable with him. It is good for young men—good for young women—that as soon as they are converted to God they should bear the yoke of service.

It is also good that when we begin to serve God we should bear the yoke in another sense, namely, *by finding difficulties.* If it were in my power to make the way of serving Christ very easy to every young Christian here, I would not do it. If it were possible to make all Sunday-school work pleasant, I would not do it. If it were possible to make standing up in the open air to preach a very easy thing, I would not make it so. It is good for you that you bear the yoke. It is good that your service should involve self-denial, and try your patience. It is good for you that the girls should not be very orderly, and that the boys should not be very teachable when you get them in the class. It is good for you that the crowd should not stand still and listen very meekly to you, and that infidels should put ugly questions to you when you are preaching in the street. It is good, I know, for the young minister to encounter curious church members, and even to meet with an adversary who means to overthrow him. It is a good thing for a true worker for the devil to labour to put him down, because if God has put him up, he cannot be put down, but the attempt to overthrow him will do him good, develop his spiritual muscle, and bring out the powers of his mind. A very easy path would not be profitable to us. Consider David after Samuel had put the oil on his head, and anointed him to be the future king of Judah ; it would have been a very bad thing for him to have waited in inglorious ease and slumbered away the interval. But take David and send him into the wilderness to keep the sheep : bring him to Saul's court, and let Saul throw a javelin at him : send him to fight with Goliath : banish him afterwards to the tracks of the wild goats, and compel him to live in the dens and in the caves and make him fight for his life, and by this process you will educate a hero, fit to rule Israel. He comes to the throne no longer a youth and ruddy, but a man of war from his youth up, and he is, therefore, ready to smite the Philistines or the children of Ammon as the champion of the Lord of Hosts. It is good, then, to bear the yoke in the sense of undertaking service for Jesus and finding difficulty in it.

And it is good yet further. *It is good to meet with persecution in your youth.* If it were possible to take every young Christian and put him into a pious family and not let him go into the world at all, but always keep him in his mother's lap—if it were possible to take every working man and guarantee that he should only work in a shop where they sing psalms from morning to night, where nobody ever swears, where nobody ever utters a word of chaff against him—why, I say, if it were possible to do this, I do not know that it would be wise to do it. To keep people out of temptation is exceedingly proper, and none of us have any right to put a temptation in another's way; but it is good for us to be tempted sometimes, otherwise we should not know the real condition of our hearts, and might be rotting with inward pride while blooming with outward morality. Temptation lets us know how weak we are, and drives us to our knees. It tests our faith and tries our love, and lets us see whether our graces are genuine or not. When religion puts on her silver slippers and walks out with her golden earrings, everybody is quite content to go with her, but the honest, hearty Christian will follow Jesus Christ's truth when she goes barefoot through the mire and through the slough, and when her garments are bespattered by unholy hands. Herein is the trial of the true, and the unmasking of the deceitful. It would not be good for us to be kept from persecution, and slander, and trial; it is good for a man that he bear this yoke in his youth. A Christian is a hardy plant. Many years ago a larch was brought to England. The gentleman who brought it put it in his hothouse, but it did not develop in a healthy manner. It was a spindly thing, and therefore the gardener, feeling that he could not make anything of it, took it up and threw it out upon the dunghill. There it grew into a splendid tree, for it had found a temperature suitable to its nature. The tree was meant to grow near the snow; it loves cold winds and rough weather, and they had been sweating it to death in a hothouse. So it is with true Christianity. It seldom flourishes so well in the midst of ease and luxury as it does in great tribulation. Christians are often all the stronger and better because they happen to be cast where they have no Christian companions, or kindly encouragements. As liberty usually favours the hardy mountaineers whose rugged hills have made them brave and hardy, so does abounding grace, as a rule, visit those who endure the great fight of affliction, and through much tribulation inherit the kingdom.

Once more, I believe it is good for young Christians to *experience much soul-trouble*. My early days of thoughtfulness were days of bitterness. Before I found a Saviour I was ploughed with the great subsoil plough of terrible convictions. Month after month I sought but found no hope. I learned the plague of my heart, the desperate evil of my nature, and at this moment I have reason to thank God for that long wintry season. I am sure it was good to my soul. As a general rule there is a period of darkness somewhere or other in the Christian life: if you have it at first it is probable you will not endure it again; but if you do not have it at first it is just as likely you will pass through the cloud at some other time. It is well to have it over. " It is good for a man that he bear the yoke in his youth." Some friends seem to have found a patent way of going to heaven. If their way is the right one I am sure I am very much delighted, but I am rather dubious, for I meet with those who have tried the high-level railroad, and are greatly discouraged because the train does not run so smoothly as they expected. They have been living a whole fortnight—well, not *quite* without sin—but very near it. They have triumphed and conquered altogether, and gone up in a balloon for a fortnight. Of course they have to come down again—and some come down with an awful fall. The best of them come, and say, " Dear pastor, I am afraid I am not a child of God. I feel so wretched, and yet I felt so happy and holy." I have said, " Yes, you see you went up, and so you had to come down. If you had *kept* down you would not have had to *come* down." That going up in a balloon to the stars frightens me about some young people; I wish they would continue humbly to feel that they are nothing and nobody, and that Christ is everything. It is much better on the whole that a man should be timid and trembling than that he should early in life become very confident. "Blessed is the man that feareth always" is a Scriptural text—not the slavish fear, nor yet a fear that doubts God, but still a fear. There is a deal of difference between doubting God and doubting yourself ; you may have as much as you like of the last till you even get to self-despair, but there 'is no reason whatever why you should doubt the Lord. " It is good for a man that he bear the yoke in his youth," to be made to feel the weight of sin, and the chastening hand of God, and to be left to cry out in the dark and say, " Oh, that I knew where I might find him, that I might come even to his seat." These ordeals are of essential service to the newborn believer, and prepare him alike for the joys and the sorrows of his spiritual career.

III. I am going to finish with this last head. Practically, brothers and sisters, WE ARE ALL OF US IN OUR YOUTH. I see some grey heads and bald heads here, and yet they belong to persons in their minority. My dear brother, though you are seventy and more, yet you have not come of age yet in the heavenly kingdom ; for if you were of age you would have your estates. None of us will come of age till we enter heaven. We are still under tutors and governors, because we are even now as little children. We have not come to that period in which we are fit for all the joys of heaven, for if we were we should be taken home to our Father's house to enjoy our inheritance at once. We are still in our youth. Well, it is good for us at this present that we should bear the yoke, and continue still to bear it. It is good, my dear brother, that we who have gone some distance on the road to heaven should still have something to bear, because it enables us to honour Christ still. If we do not suffer with him, how can we have fellowship with him ? If we have no crosses to carry, how can we commune with our Lord, the chief cross-bearer ? Let us be glad that we are not spared tribulation, that we are not screened from affliction, but are permitted to glorify God by patience, by resignation, and by unstaggering faith. Do not ask the Lord that you may have no trouble, but rather remember you have only a little while in which you can be patient—only a little while in which you can be a cross-bearer, and therefore it behoves you to use each moment well. A few more revolving suns and you will be where there is no more cross to carry, no sorrow to bear, and, therefore, where there is no room for patience, and no opportunity of being acquiescent in the divine will. Be content to bear the yoke now, for it is but a little while, and this honour will be no longer yours,

It is good for us all to bear the yoke, too, because thus *old Adam is kept in check.* A wonderfully vivacious thing is that old Adam. He has been reported to be dead a good many times, but to my certain knowledge he is very brisk still. When we are in trouble, proud old Adam often seems to be quiet, and does not so well succeed in keeping us from prayer; and, consequently, in times of trouble, we often enjoy our very sweetest seasons of devotion. By the Lord's goodness we escape the trial, but, alas, old Adam soon lifts up his proud head again. He says, " Ah, you are a favourite of heaven, your mountain standeth firm. Your affliction has been sanctified to you, and you have grown in grace very wonderfully. The fact is, you are a very fine fellow." Yes, that is old Adam's way, and whenever he sees an opportunity he will return to his old game of flattery. Whenever you are tempted to be vain, say to yourself, " I know you, old Adam. I know you, and will not yield to your crafty devices." What happens when we become self-satisfied? Why, the yoke returns upon our shoulders heavily again. We fall into another trouble, and then old Adam is up in the stirrups again, and begins to grumble and rebel. The flesh begins proudly to despair, whereas a little while before it was boasting. Trials, in the hands of the Spirit, are a great help to overcome corruptions. It is a very hard matter for a man to be rich and prospering in this world, to be at ease and have a long stretch of health, and to have everything go exactly as he likes, and yet to be a Christian. When the road is very smooth many fall, but when the way is rough there is good grip for the feet, and we are not so likely to stumble. When trials come, they whip us home to our heavenly Father. Sheep do not stray so much when the black dog is after them; his barkings make them run to the shepherd. Affliction is the black dog of the Good Shepherd to fetch us back to him, otherwise we should wander to our ruin. We are not better than David; and we may honestly confess as he did, " Before I was afflicted I went astray, but now have I kept thy word." Therefore it is good for us spiritually young people, even though old as to the flesh, that we should bear the yoke while we are still in our youth.

Besides, dear friends, it makes you so *helpful to others* to have known affliction. I do not see how we can sympathize if we are never tried ourselves. I know a beloved brother who is perhaps fifty years of age, who never had a day's sickness, and he told me he scarcely knew what physical pain was except when a heavy person trod on his toes. Well, now, he is a good brother; but when he tries to sympathize, it is like an elephant picking up a pin, or Hercules with a distaff; he does do it, but it is a thing to be wondered at. If you tell him that you feel very low in spirits, he looks at you and tries to say very kind things, but he does not understand your despondency. Now, it would be a great pity for a Christian minister to be lacking in the power to sympathize—would it not? Oh, thank God for troubles, because they make the heart tender, and they teach the lips the art of consolation. You can be a Boanerges without trouble, but you never can be a Barnabas; you may be a son of thunder, but you will never be a son of consolation. As we wish to serve others, let us thank God that he qualifies us to do so by making us bear the yoke in our youth.

Once more, is it not good to bear the yoke while we are here, because *it will make heaven all the sweeter?* Oh, how sweet heaven will be to that bedridden woman, who has lain these twenty years upon her weary couch, and scarcely had a night's unbroken rest! What rest heaven will be to her! I know a good man within two miles of this place who has laid eighteen years without moving. I do not know a happier man than he is. It is a treat to see him; but still what a change it will be, from that bed from which he cannot rise, to stand on the sea of glass, and for ever wave the palm branch, and draw forth music from the celestial harp. What a transformation! How great the change for a poor Christian woman dying in a workhouse, to be carried by angels into Abraham's bosom! What a change for the martyr standing at the stake burning slowly to death, and then rising to behold the glory of his Lord! What a change for you, dear old friend, with all those aches and pains about you, which make you feel uneasy even while you are sitting here! Ah, greybeard, you will be young soon. There will be no wrinkles on your brow. You will not require those spectacles; you will not need that staff to lean upon; you will be as strong as the youngest there. As you stand before the throne of God you will scarcely know yourself to be the same old woman you used to be, or the same sickly man you were a little while ago. You will be stripped of the house of clay, and your young soul will leap up from the old body and be present with the Lord; and then the grave will be a fining pot in which the dross of the flesh will be consumed; and by-and-by your body will rise, no longer old and haggard and worn, but full of beauty, like your Master's glorious body. This should give joy to you at all times: it must be good for you to bear the yoke, seeing heaven will by that means be made more fully heaven to you when once you reach its everlasting rest.

> "The way may be rough, but it cannot be long;
>   So let's smooth it with hope, and cheer it with song."

5 An Anxious Inquiry for a Beloved Son

"And the king said, Is the young man Absalom safe?"—2 Samuel xviii. 29.

THIS was said by David after a great battle in which many had been slain, and the hosts led by Absalom had fallen to the number of twenty thousand; perishing not only by the sword, but among the thick oaks and tangled briers of the wood, which concealed fearful precipices and great caverns, into which the rebels plunged in their wild fright when the rout set in. His father's anxious question concerned his wicked but still well-beloved son, "Is the young man Absalom safe?" He does not appear to have asked, "How have we won the victory?" but "Is the young man Absalom safe?" Not "Is Joab, the captain of my host, alive, for upon him so much depends?" but "Is the young man Absalom safe?" Not "How many of our noble troops have fallen in the battle?" but "Is the young man Absalom safe?" It has been said that he showed here more of the father than of the king—more of affection than of wisdom; and that is, doubtless, a correct criticism upon the old man's absorbing fondness. David was no doubt, in this case, weak in his excessive tenderness. But, brethren, it is much more easy for us to blame a father under such circumstances than for us quite to understand his feelings; I may add, it would be wiser to sympathize, as far as we can, than to sit in judgment upon a case which has never been our own. Perhaps if we were placed in the same position we should find it impossible to feel otherwise than he did. How many there are at this present moment who have, no doubt, other very weighty businesses, but whose one only thought just now is, "Is the young man safe? Is my son safe? Is my father safe? Is my wife safe?" A vessel has gone down in the river with hundreds on board, and weeping friends are going hither and thither from place to place, hoping and yet fearing to identify the corpse of some beloved one; longing to find one who has not been heard of since the fatal hour, and trembling all the while lest they should find him or her among the bodies which have been drawn from the cold stream. The one thought uppermost with scores to-night is this one—" Is my beloved one safe?" Do you blame them? They are neglecting business, and forsaking their daily toil, but do you blame them? A hundred weighty things are forgotten in the one eager enquiry: do you, can you, blame them? Assuredly not. It is natural, and it is therefore, I think, but right. Though, no doubt, David did afterwards show a measure of petulance and of rebellion against God, and is not altogether to be commended, yet who that has a father's heart within him would not rather undertake to justify than to censure the aged parent? When the old man asks concerning his son, " Is the young man Absalom safe?" and, finding that he is not, cries, " O my son Absalom, my son, my son Absalom! would God I had died for thee, O Absalom, my son, my son!" we would not, like Joab, go in to him and coarsely upbraid him, however much he might deserve it, but we would rather sit down and weep in sympathy with those that feel a kindred anxiety, and see if we may not learn something from their sorrow. If our own anxieties are free in that direction, let us turn them in some other direction which may be really useful, and tend to the glory of God.

Let us first, to-night, consider for a little *this question of anxiety*, then *think of occasions for its use*, and then, thirdly, *suggest answers which may be given to it*.

I. First, let us think of THIS QUESTION OF ANXIETY—" Is the young man Absalom safe?"

And the first remark is, *it is a question asked by a father concerning his son*. " Is he safe?" The anxieties of parents are very great, and some young people do not sufficiently reflect upon them, or they would be more grateful, and would not so often increase them by their thoughtless conduct. I am persuaded that there are many sons and daughters who would not willingly cost their parents sorrow, who, nevertheless, do flood their lives with great grief. It cannot always be innocently that they do this: there must be a measure of wanton wrong about it in many cases where young people clearly foresee the result of their conduct upon their friends. There are some young men, especially, who in the indulgence of what they call their freedom trample on the tender feelings of her that bare them, and frequently cause sleepless nights and crushing troubles to both their parents. This is a crime to be answered for before the bar of God, who has given a special promise to dutiful children, and reserves a special curse for rebellious ones. All parents must have anxieties. There is never a babe dropped into a mother's bosom but it brings care, labour, grief, and anxiety with it. There is a joy in the parental relationship, but there must necessarily be a vast amount of anxious care with it throughout those tender years of infancy in which the frail cockle-shell boat of life seems likely to be swamped by a thousand waves which sweep harmlessly over stronger barques. The newly-lit candle is so readily blown out that mothers nurse and watch with a care which frequently saps the parental life. But our children, perhaps, do not give us most anxiety when they are infants, nor when we have them at school, when we can put them to bed and give them a good-night's kiss and feel that all is safe ; the heavy care comes afterwards—afterwards when they have broken through our control, when they are running alone, and on their own account, when they are away from our home, when they are out of the reach of our rebuke, and do not now feel as once they did the power of our authority, and hardly of our love. It is then to many parents that the time of severe trial begins, and, doubtless, many a grey head has been brought with sorrow to the grave by having to cry, " I have nourished and brought up children, and they have rebelled against me." Many a father and many a mother die, murdered, not with knife or poison, but by unkind words and cruel deeds of their own children. Many and many a grave may well be watered by the tears of sons and daughters, because they prematurely filled those graves by their ungrateful conduct. Let us all think, who still have parents spared to us, how much we owe to them, and let it be our joy, if we cannot recompense them, at any rate to give them so much of comfort by our conduct as shall show our gratitude. Let them have such joy in us that they may never regret the anxieties of past years, but may have their hearts made to rejoice that they brought into the world such sons and daughters. If we have had parents who did care for us, and anxiously said, "Are they safe?" let us be grateful to God, and let us never show that we undervalue his mercy by treating the boon with contempt.

Secondly, *this was a question asked about a son who had left his father's house.* "Is the young man Absalom safe?" As I have already said, we have not so much anxiety about our children when they are at home and when the nursery holds them as we have afterwards when they are beyond our reach. They have formed their own attachments, and have commenced life entirely on their own account. Even if they are in the same town, we are concerned for their welfare ; but if they are in another land, we have still more anxious thoughts. Possibly some of you have your sons and daughters far removed from you, and I do not doubt that, if it be so, you often start at night with the question, "How fares it with my boy? How is it with my son?" He is far away there, an emigrant, or a sailor at sea, or in some distant country town engaged in earning his livelihood, and you wonder whether he is alive and well. If you know him to be on shore, you would fain know whether he goes regularly to the house of God on the Sabbath-day. You wonder where he spends his evenings. You wonder into what sort of company he may have fallen, what sort of master or shopmates he lives with, and what are the influences of his home. I am quite sure that such anxious questions frequently plough deep furrows across your minds. There are some young men here to-night, in London, come to live in our great city, and I want kindly to remind them of the tender thoughts about them at home—how mother and father, perhaps at this very hour, are thinking of them and praying for them. They would be glad, probably, to know that their son is where he is, but they might have sorrow if they knew where sometimes he wastes his evenings, and where he has begun to spend a part of his Sabbath-day. They would be grieved to know that he is beginning to forget the habits formed at home—that now in the room where there are others sleeping he is afraid to bow his knee in prayer—that the Bible in which his mother wrote his name, and concerning which the promise was given that there should be a portion read every day has not been read, but some book of very doubtful character has taken its place. Young friend, some of us who are a little older know your experience of leaving home, and we trust you will know our experience of having been followed by the prayers and tears of parents who have lived to rejoice that their prayers for us were abundantly answered. May it be so in your case, for, if not, you will go from bad to worse and perish in your sin. Yet it is very hard for a young man to go down to hell, riding steeple-chase over a mother's prayers. It takes a great deal of energy to damn yourself when a father and a mother are pleading for your salvation, and yet there are some who accomplish it; and, when they come into the place of ruin and destruction, surely there shall be a heavier measure meted out to them than to those who were trained in the gutter and tutored in the street, and never knew what it was to be the subjects of parental prayer. O Lord Jesus, thou who didst raise the widow's dead son, save those sons who are dead in trespasses and in sins, who are even now being carried out to be buried in the tomb of vice and corruption.

"Is the young man Absalom safe?" may very readily remind us of the anxieties of Christian parents about their sons and daughters when they are away from home.

But there is a touching point about this. *It is the question of a father about his rebellious son.* Absalom—the young man Absalom—why should David be concerned about him? Was he not up in arms against him? Did he not thirst for his father's blood? Was he not at the head of a vast host, seeking anxiously to slay his father, that he might wear his crown, which he had already usurped. Why, methinks, he might have said, "Is the young man Absalom dead? for if he is out of the way there will be peace to my realm, and rest to my troubled life." But no, he is a father, and he must love his own offspring. It is a father that speaks, and a father's love can survive the enmity of a son. He can live on and love on even when his son seeks his heart's blood. What a noble passion is a mother's love or a father's love! It is an image in miniature of the love of God. How reverently ought we to treat it! How marvellously has God been pleased to endow, especially godly people, with the sacred instinct of affection towards their children, an instinct which God sanctifies to noblest ends. Our children may plunge into the worst of sins, but they are our children still. They may scoff at our God; they may tear our heart to pieces with their wickedness; we cannot take complacency in them, but at the same time we cannot unchild them, nor erase their image from our hearts. We do earnestly remember them still, and shall do so as long as these hearts of ours shall beat within our bosoms. I have now and then met with professing Christians who have said, "That girl shall never darken my door again." I do not believe in their Christianity. Whenever I have met with fathers who are irreconcilable to their children, I am convinced that they are unreconciled to God. It cannot be possible that there should exist in us a feeling of enmity to our own offspring after our hearts have been renewed; for if the Lord has forgiven *us*, and received *us* into his family, surely we can forgive the chief of those

who have offended us; and when they are our own flesh and blood we
are doubly bound to do so. To cast off our own children is unnatural,
and that which is unnatural cannot be gracious. If even publicans and
sinners forgive their children, much more must we. Let them go even
to extremities of unheard-of sin, yet as the mercy of God endureth for
ever, so must the love of a Christian parent still endure. If David says,
"Is the young man Absalom safe?" we have none of us had a son that
has acted one half so badly as Absalom; and we must, therefore, still
forgive and feel a loving interest in those who grieve us.

At this time I would address any young person who has been a great
grief to those at home? Do you treat this matter lightly? Do your
parents' anxieties seem to you to be foolishness? Ah, let me remind
you that though your course of life may be sport to you, it is death to
those at home. You may dry up your heart towards your mother, but
your mother's heart still overflows with love to you. You may even
count it a joke that you have caused her tears; but those tears are
sincere, and reveal her inward agony of soul. Can you ridicule such
tender affection? I have known some young people who have fallen so
low as to have made mockery of their parents' piety. It is a horrible
thing to do, and woe unto those who have been guilty of it. Yet many
Christian parents only return prayers and greater affection for such
unkindness as this, and still go on to lay their children's case before
God, and beseech him for his mercy's sake to have mercy upon them.
Now, erring young man, since there is something human remaining in
you, I appeal to your tenderer nature that you will not continue to
offend against such marvellous love, and will not wantonly go on to
trample on such patient forgiveness. Absalom, if he could have heard
his father ask the question, "Is the young man Absalom safe?" was, I
doubt not, bad enough still to have rebelled against him; but I hope
it is not so with anyone here; nay, I trust that when the most wilful
shall see the deep and true love of their parents' hearts they will hasten
to be reconciled to them, and spend the rest of their lives in undoing
the ill which they have done.

The question of my text is the question of a parent concerning *a son
who, if he were not safe, but dead, was certainly in a very dreadful plight.*
"Is the young man Absalom safe?" said David, with all the deeper
earnestness because he felt that if he was not alive he was in an evil
case. He has died red-handed in rebellion against his father—into
what shades must his guilty soul have descended? O beloved, that
is a very serious question to ask about any departed person. Where
is he? Is his soul safe? I could almost pray that, when any die
by sudden death, they might be God's people, and that the sinners
might escape till they have found Christ. We admire that Christian
man who, finding himself with another at the bottom of a coal
pit, was about to ascend in the cage. There was only a chance for
one, for the basket would hold no more. He had taken his place, but
he left it, and said to the other miner, "My soul is saved; I am a believer in Christ. You are not. If you die you are a lost man. Jump
into the cage." Thus he allowed his unconverted companion to escape,
and ventured his own life in his stead. If we are ourselves in Christ,
it would be Christlike to be ready to die instead of the unsaved;

then should we carry out David's wish—"Would God I had died for thee." To die—the bitterness of death is passed where there is a good hope through grace; but for those to die who have no hope, no Christ, no heaven—this is death indeed. I can very well imagine any of you asking very seriously about your sons and daughters, "Are they safe?" when you know that if they have been suddenly taken away they were altogether unprepared. If men and women are unconverted when they die they will die twice, and the second death is the most to be feared. Are not some of you, my hearers, in such danger? Dear friends, where would you be suppose at this moment the blast of death were to pass through this house and chill your very marrow? If, now, the secret arrow must find a target in some one bosom, where would you be if it should be ordained for you? Do ask yourself the question, and, if you have no hope in Christ, God help you to seek and find forgiveness by the precious blood of Jesus.

Yet, once more, *this was a question, alas! which was asked by a father about a son who was really dead at the time when the question was asked.* It was late in the day to enquire for Absalom's safety; for it was all over with that rebellious son. The three darts of Joab had gone through the very heart of Absalom, and there, hanging by its hair in the oak, his body dangled between earth and heaven. He had already been justly executed for his crimes, and yet his father asked, "Is the young man Absalom safe?" It is too late to ask questions about our children when they are dead. I should think that David's heart must have been pierced with many sorrows at the thought of his own negligence of his children, for there are hints in his life which lead us to fear that, if not altogether an Eli, he was far too negligent in the matter of household management. We read of one son of his that his father had never denied him anything, and I can hardly imagine a man to be a good father of whom that could be said concerning any one of his sons. The practice of polygamy is altogether destructive of proper family discipline, and David had erred greatly in that respect; besides which he was so occupied with public affairs, that his sons were allowed too great a liberty. And now he is vainly asking "Is the young man Absalom safe?" The question is too late. It is of no use to wring your hands if your boy has grown up to be a debauchee and a drunkard: train him while he is yet young, and bring him with your prayers and tears to Christ while yet a child. Mother, it will little avail you to tear your hair because of a daughter's dishonour if you have permitted her to go into society where temptations abound. Let us do for our children what we can do for them *while* they are little ones. While the warm metal flows, as it were, soft and plastic, let us try to turn it into the right mould: for if it once grows cold, we may beat it in vain, it will not take the desired image and superscription. Oh that those of us who have little children about us may have grace to train them up in the way they should go, for when they are old they will not depart from it. You cannot bend the tree, but you can twist the sapling: look ye well to it. Snatch the opportunity while yet it is before you, lest, when your children have plunged into sin, or may even have plunged into the pit, you vex your souls in vain and cry, "Woe is me." I shall never forget the anguish of a poor illiterate woman whom I had been the means of leading to Christ. She was rejoicing in Christ when I had seen her before, but when I saw her next she was in great sorrow and bondage of spirit, and I said to her, "What aileth thee?" She replied, "My children! my children! They are all grown up, and they are all ungodly. My husband died and left me a widow with five or six of them. I worked hard morning and night, as you know I must have done, to find them clothes and food; and I brought them up as well as I could; but, woe's me, I never thought about their souls. How could I?" said she, "for I never thought about my own; and now I am saved, but they are all worldly and care-less, and I cannot undo the mischief." She told me that, touched with a feeling of love to her children, she had resolved to go and speak to each of them about their eternal state; and she made her first visit to her eldest son, who had a family of children around him, and when she began to tell him about her conversion and her salvation and joy in the Lord, he so cruelly laughed her to scorn that it broke her heart. I did all I could to cheer and comfort her; but I can only say to younger persons, who are converted whilst still they have their little ones about them, never let the occasion go, lest you have to cry out at last, "O Absalom, my son, my son Absalom! would God I had died for thee, O Absalom, my son! for thou hast fallen in thy iniquity, and it may be thy blood will be required at thy parent's hands." God grant that this question of anxiety may be asked in time by wise parents, and not left till its answer shall smite as doth a dagger.

II. Secondly. You have had the question; we are now to speak upon SOME OCCASIONS WHEN THAT QUESTION WOULD VERY NATURALLY BE USED. "Is the young man Absalom safe?"

The question would be used, of course, in times, like the present, *in reference to this mortal life.* When a fearful calamity has swept away hundreds at a stroke such an enquiry is on every lip. On Wednesday morning how many families must have looked down those fearful lists, having been up all night watching and waiting for some one who did not come home. What a dreadful night to spend in watching for son or father, or daughter or mother; and how awful the tidings of the morn-ing! In the case of a family near my own house, the servant was left at home with one little babe, and all the rest of the family went out for a day's pleasure and health-seeking. Nobody has ever come home! No-body has come to relieve the servant and embrace the child! You may imagine the anxiety of that servant with her little charge, to find master and mistress and the rest never coming home. There is also a case of a mother upstairs with a new-born little one at her side, and her husband and her other children, who had gone out, never returned. May we never know such sorrow! Then is the question asked in accents of terror, "Is the young man Absalom safe?"

Times of disease, also, raise such enquiries. Well do I recollect some four-and-twenty years ago, when first I came to London, it was my painful duty to go, not only by day, but by night, from house to house where the cholera was raging; and almost every time I met the beloved friends at Park Street it was my sorrow to hear it said, "Mr. So-and-so is dead. Mistress A. or B. is gone," till I sickened myself from very grief.

It was then most natural that each one should say concerning his relative at a little distance, "Is he still alive? Is he still safe?"

Now, if in any future day the shadow of a disaster should cross your path, and you should be in fear that your beloved ones are lost, I pray you, if you are Christian people, exercise faith at such a time, and stay yourselves upon God. Recollect, if you become so anxious as to lose your clearness of mind, you will not be fit for the emergency. It may be that by retaining calmness of soul you will be of service; but by giving up the very helm of your mind, and allowing yourself to drift before the torrent of anxiety, you will become useless and helpless. In patience possess your souls. The world is in God's hand after all. The young man Absalom will not die without the appointment of heaven. Your children are not out of the keeping of the Most High. However dear they are to you, and however great their peril, there is One that ruleth and overruleth; and quiet prayer has more power with him than impatient fretfulness. If your dear ones are dead you cannot restore them to life by your unbelief; and if they still survive, it will be a pity to be downcast and unbelieving when there is no occasion for it. "Your strength is to sit still." Remember that you are a Christian, and a Christian is expected to be more self-possessed than those who have no God to fly to. The holy self-composedness of faith is one of the things which recommend it to the outside world, and men who see Christian men and women calm, when others are beside themselves, are led to ask, "What is this?" and unconsciously to own, "This is the finger of God." So when you ask the painful question before us, ask it still with faith in God.

But, dear friends, sometimes we have to ask this question about friends and children, *with regard to their eternal life.* They are dead, and we are fearful that they did not die in Christ, and therefore we enquire, "Is the young man Absalom safe?" It is very painful to the Christian minister when that question is put to him, and it is not for him to answer it in most cases. As a rule he knows too little of the person to form a judgment. He may, perhaps, have paid a visit or two, and he may have been encouraged by a few hopeful words: but what can we judge from a dying-bed? It is very easy for a dying person to be deceived and to deceive others, and we had better leave judgments and decisions in the hand of God. Those who know all about the person's life, and have been in the chamber all the time of his sickness, and know more, how should they judge? I answer, where there has been no previous godly life, where the conversion must have been a very late one, and the signs and marks of it are feeble—*judge hopefully, but judge honestly.* You are allowed to hope, but still be honest, and avoid, above all things, the unwisdom I have seen in some people of holding up a son or a daughter or a friend for an example, when the individual has lived an ungodly life, and never showed the slightest sign of grace while in active life, but merely used a pious expression or two at the last. Hope if you dare, but be very careful of what you say. To parade the few last words as if they had more weight in them than a long life cast into the other scale is very unwise. It is most injurious to the rest of the family, and is apt to make them feel that they may live as they like, and yet be considered saints when they die. I rather admire, though

I might not imitate, a father who, on the contrary, when his ungodly son died, said to his sons and daughters, "My dear children, much as I wish I could have any hope about your brother, his whole life was so inconsistent with anything like that of a Christian, that I fear he is lost for ever. I must warn you earnestly not to live as he lived, lest you should die as he died." There was honesty in such dealing, honesty to be admired. If you must judge and answer the question, "Is the young man Absalom safe?" be not so hopeful as to deceive yourselves and others, and be not so severe as to constitute yourselves judges upon a matter in which you can know, after all, but little, unless the whole life has been before you. In that case you may judge with some degree of certainty, for it is written, "By their fruits shall ye know them."

"Is the young man Absalom safe?" is a more practical question when we put it about young people and old people, when they are still alive, and we are anxious about *their spiritual condition.* "Is the young man Absalom safe?" That is to say, is he really safe for the future?—for this world and for the world to come. We saw him in the enquiry-room, we heard him speak out his anxiety, and we marked his tears; but is he safe? Not if he stops there. We have seen him since then at the house of God amongst the most earnest hearers. He leans forward to catch every syllable : he is evidently in earnest; but is he safe? Not if he stops there. He is a seeker: there can be no doubt about it. He has now begun to read his Bible, and he endeavours to draw near to God in prayer. Is he safe? Not if he stops even there. He must come to faith in Jesus Christ and really cast himself upon the great atonement made by the redeeming blood, or else he is not safe. The question for you Sunday-school teachers to ask about your children is, Are they *safe?* Have they reached the point in which they turn from darkness to light—from the power of Satan to the power of Christ? "Is the young man Absalom *safe?*" Is he *saved?* That is the point.

I believe there is a denomination of Christians who receive into membership those *who desire to be saved.* I will not judge such a plan, but I dare not follow it. To *desire* to be saved is a very simple matter, and means little. The point is to *be* saved. That is the question, and over it all our anxiety should be expended. "Is the young man Absalom "—not hopeful, not aroused or convicted, but is he " safe"? Is he saved in the Lord with an everlasting salvation? Hear it all of you, and answer for yourselves.

III. The third point is to be THE ANSWERS WHICH WE HAVE TO GIVE TO THIS QUESTION—" Is the young man Absalom safe?"

This question has often been sent up by friends from the country about their lads who have come to London—"Is my boy Harry safe? Is my son John safe?" Answer, sometimes : "No, no. He is not safe. We are sorry to say that he is in great danger." I will tell you when we know he is not safe.

He is not safe if, like Absalom, he is at enmity with his father. Oh, no. He may attend a place of worship, and he may profess to pray, and he may even take upon himself the name of a Christian; but he is not safe if he is at enmity with his parents. That will not do at all.

Scripture saith, " If a man love not his brother whom he hath seen, how can he love God whom he hath not seen?" The words are quite as forcible if we read father instead of brother. If a man love not his own parents on earth, how can he love his Father who is in heaven? No, no; he is not safe.

"Is the young man safe?" Well, no. We have seen him lately in bad company. He has associated with other young men who are of loose morals. He prefers to spend his evenings where there may be bare decency in the songs and the conversation, but scarcely more. No, the young man Absalom is not safe there. He may be very moral himself, but he will not long remain pure if he goes into such society. If you sit among coals, if you do not burn yourself, you will blacken yourself. If you choose bad company, if you are not absolutely made to transgress as they do, yet you will damage your reputation. No, the young man Absalom is not safe.

And he is not safe, because he has taken to indulge in expensive habits. "Absalom prepared him," it is said, "chariots and horses, and fifty men to run before him." This extravagance was a sign of evil. A youth who lavishes money upon needless luxuries is not safe. Certain young men of London, with small salaries, manage to cut a superb figure, and we fear that something wrong lies behind it. Their plain but honest and respected fathers certainly would not know them if they were to see them in full array. It is a bad sign when young men go in for dash and show beyond their position and means. Of course, every man's expenditure must be regarded with reference to his income and station in life. I am not touching upon the style of men of rank and fortune, though even there a vain-glorious appearance is the index of evil; but there are some young fellows scarcely out of their teens, or who have scarcely ended their apprenticeships, whose pocket-money must be easy to count, who nevertheless indulge themselves in all sorts of extravagances, and when I see them doing so I feel sure that the " young man Absalom" is not safe.

Another thing. The young man Absalom is not safe, as you may see, if you look at his personal appearance. We read, "But in all Israel there was none to be so much praised as Absalom for his beauty : from the sole of his foot even to the crown of his head there was no blemish in him. And when he polled his head, (for it was at every year's end that he polled it : because the hair was heavy on him, therefore he polled it :) he weighed the hair of his head at two hundred shekels after the king's weight." When young people are taken up with their own persons, and are vain of their hair, their looks, and their dress, we are sure that they are not safe, for pride is always in danger. Let young men and women dress according to their stations ; we are not condemning them for that. I recollect Mr. Jay saying, " If you ladies will tell me your income to a penny, I will tell you how many ribbons you may wear to a yard"; and I think that I might venture to say the same. But I do notice that when young people begin to be vain of their beauty and fond of dress they are in great peril from various kinds of temptations. There is a canker-worm somewhere in their brain or their heart that will eat up their good resolutions and fair characters. No, the young man with his boasted beauty is not safe.

And we are sure the young man Absalom is not safe, when he has begun to be vicious. You recollect what Absalom did : I need not go into particulars. Now, many a young man, albeit he is not reckoned a bad fellow, has still gone astray in private life, and if all secrets were laid bare, he would be almost ashamed to sit among respectable people who now receive him into their society. No, he is not safe.

"Is the young man Absalom safe?" No, David, he is not, for the last time we saw him he was in a battle, and the people were dying all around him, and therefore he is not safe. How can he be safe where others fall? Yes, and I saw the young man come out of a low place of amusement late one night, and I thought, "No, the young man Absalom is not safe," for many perish there. I heard of his betting at the races, and I thought, "The young man Absalom is not safe, for multitudes are ruined there." I saw him in loose company one evening, and I said, "No, the young man Absalom is not safe : he is surrounded by those who hunt for the precious life." It is never safe for us to be where other people fall; because if they perish, why should not we? The youth did not see this, but answered me fiercely when I pointed out his danger. He said that he knew how to keep himself : it was not to be taken for granted, because he was going in for amusements, that he would become vicious. "Of course," said he, "there are young fellows who cannot take care of themselves, but I am quite able to look after myself. I can put on the drag whenever I please ; I am gay, but I am not bad ; I am free, but not vicious." Yes, but I wrote down, "The young man Absalom is not safe"—not half so safe as he thinks he is— and all the less safe, because he thinks so much of himself, and is so particularly sure that he can conquer where other people perish. No, the young man Absalom is not safe.

Now, the young man is here to-night who will answer to the next description. He is a very nice young fellow. All of us who know him love him and are right glad to see him among us. He is a great hearer and lover of the gospel word, *but he is not decided.* He has never taken his stand with God's people, confessing Christ as his Lord. "Almost thou persuadest me to be a Christian," he has often said ; but he is not quite persuaded yet. Is the young man safe? Oh, no. He is very hopeful, God bless him ! We will pray him into safety if we can ; but he is not safe yet. Those people who were almost saved from the wreck of the *Princess Alice* were drowned ; and those persons who are almost saved from sin are still lost. If you are almost alive you are dead ; if you are almost forgiven you are under condemnation ; if you are almost regenerated you are unregenerate; if you are almost a Christian you are without God and without hope, and if you die almost saved you will be altogether lost.

O my dear young brother, I wish that I could answer and say, "Yes, the young man Absalom is safe : he has taken the decisive step, he has resigned himself into the hands of Jesus, and Jesus will keep him to the end." May the Holy Ghost lead you to this.

A pleasant task remains, I will now answer that question with a happy "Yes." Yes, the young man Absalom is safe.

Why? Well, first, because he is a believer in Christ. He has cast himself upon Jesus. He knew that he could not save himself, and so he came to Christ that Christ might save him, and he has left himself entirely in the hands of Jesus to be his for ever and ever.

The young man is saved, for he loves the gospel. He will not go to hear anything but the gospel. He sticks to the truth, he knows the unadulterated milk of the Word, and he cannot be deceived and led astray with false doctrine, for that he hates. He does not gad about to go and hear this and that, but he knows what has saved his soul, and he holds fast the form of sound words. The young man is safe.

I know he is safe, for he is very humble. He is not perfect yet: he does not say that he is, nor boast of his attainments. He does not want to be the forehorse of the team, he is willing to be placed anywhere so that he can be useful. He often wonders that he is a Christian at all, and ascribes it all to divine grace. He is a lowly young man, and therefore he is safe enough, for such the Lord preserveth.

Moreover, he is very diffident of himself. He is afraid sometimes to put one foot before another for fear he should take a wrong step. He is always going on his knees to ask for direction; he waits upon God for guidance, and does not dare to do anything without the direction of the word and the Spirit. He is a prayerful man, and therefore he is safe; for who can hurt the man who dwells at the mercy-seat? He is also a very careful man in his daily walk. He labours to be obedient to the will of God, he aims at being holy, and to be holy is to be safe.

Worldlings say that he is a cant and a hypocrite, and thus they have set their stamp on him, and marked him as a follower of the despised Redeemer. He is a genuine character, or else they would not persecute him. The people of God love him, and he loves them, and he dwells among them, and says of the house of God,

> "Here my best friends, my kindred dwell,
> Here God my Saviour reigns."

Write home to his father and all his friends, and say, "The young man is safe." He is in Christ, and he is in Christ's church, and he is seeking to serve God. He is beginning to work for the Master, he is trying to bring souls to Jesus; the Holy Spirit is working in him and by him to the glory of God. Yes, he is safe enough, for he is "Safe in the arms of Jesus."

6 A Description of Young Men in Christ

"I write unto you, young men, because ye have overcome the wicked one. . . . I have written unto you, young men, because ye are strong, and the word of God abideth in you, and ye have overcome the wicked one."—1 John ii. 13, 14.

WHEN I preached a short time ago upon John's message to the "little children," I explained why it was that he first said, "I write," and then, "I have written." He is writing : his whole heart is in it, and he cannot help saying that he himself is earnestly writing to those whom he loves so well; but he has scarcely penned the line before he feels that he must alter that present tense and set it in the past, under the form of "I have written." He knows that he must soon be gone from them, and be numbered with those who were, but are not, among living men. These words, then, are the language of a father in Israel still among his children ; they are also the words of one who has passed from earth and entered into glory. If what I shall have to say at this time, fairly flowing from the text, shall come to you as Christ's word from his favoured disciple John you will attach the more importance to it, and it will do your hearts the more good. Lifting his head from that dear bosom which gave him unexampled rest he whispers, " I write unto you young men." Looking down from that favoured place which he now occupies so near to the throne of the Lamb, he looks over the battlements of heaven upon us, and cries, "I have written unto you, young men."

In the Christian church there is an order of Christians who have grown so much that they can no longer be called " babes in grace," but yet they are not so far matured that they can be exactly called " fathers." These, who form the middle-class of the spiritual-minded, are styled "young men." Understand that the apostle is not writing here to any according to their bodily age ; he is using human age as a metaphor and figure for representing growth in the spiritual life. Age, according to the flesh, often differs much from the condition of the spirit : many old men are still no more than " babes "; some children in years are even now " young men " in grace, while not a few young men are " fathers " in the church while young in years. God has endowed certain of his servants with great grace, and made them mature in their youth : such were Joseph, Samuel, David, Josiah, and Timothy. It is not age according to the family register that we are now to speak about, but age according to the Lamb's book of life.

Grace is a matter of growth, and hence we have among us babes, young men, and fathers, whose position is not reckoned according to this fleeting, dying. life, but according to that eternal life which has been wrought in them of the Spirit of God. It is a great mercy when young men in the natural sense are also young men in the spiritual sense, and I am glad that it is largely so in this church. The fathers among us need not be ashamed of their spiritual seed. In speaking to young men in Christ, I am speaking to a numerous body of Christians among ourselves, who make up a very efficient part of the army of Christ in this region. I would ask them not to be either so modest or so proud as to decline to be thus classed. You are no longer weaklings; do not, therefore, count yourselves mere babes, lest you plead exemption from hard service. You are hardly yet mature enough to rank with the fathers; do not forget the duties of your real place under cover of aspiring to another. It is honour enough to be in Christ, and certainly it is no small thing to be in spiritual things a man in the prime of life.

These young men are not babes. They have been in Christ too long for that: they are no longer novices, to whom the Lord's house is strange. They have been born unto God probably now for years: the things which they hoped for at first they have to a large extent realized; they know now what once they could not understand. They are not now confined to milk diet; they can eat meat and digest it well. They have discernment, having had their senses exercised by reason of use, so that they are not so liable to be misled as they were in their infancy. And while they have been longer in the way, so also have they now grown stronger in the way. It is not a weak and timorous faith which they now possess; they believe firmly and stoutly, and are able to do battle for the "faith once delivered to the saints," for they are strong in the Lord and in the power of his might. They are wiser now than they used to be. When they were children they knew enough to save them, for they knew the Father, and that was blessed knowledge; but now they know far more of the word of God which abideth in them through their earnest, prayerful, believing reception of it. Now they have a clearer idea of the breadth and length, and depth and height of the work of redemption, for they have been taught of God. They even venture to enjoy the deep things of God; and the covenant is by no means an unknown thing among them. They have been under the blessed teaching of the Spirit of God, and from him they have received an unction, so that they know all things. In knowledge they are no more children, but men in Christ Jesus. Thus they are distinguished from the first class, which comprehends the babes in Christ.

They are not yet fathers because they are not yet so established, confirmed, and settled as the fathers are, who know what they believe, and know it with a certainty of full assurance which nothing can shake. They have not yet had the experience of fathers, and consequently have not all their prudence and foresight: they are richer in zeal than in judgment. They have not yet acquired the nursing faculty so precious in the church as the product of growth, experience, maturity, and affection; they are going on to that, and in a short time they will have reached it, but as yet they have other work to do more suitable to their vigour. Do not suppose that when we say they are not to be called "fathers," that they are not, therefore, very valuable to the community; for in some senses they are quite equal to the fathers, and in one or two respects they may even be superior to them. The fathers are for contemplation, they study deep and see far, and so they "have known him that is from the beginning"; but a measure of their energy for action may have gone through stress of years. These young men are born to fight; they are the militia of the church, they have to contend for her faith, and to extend the Redeemer's kingdom. They should do so, for they are strong. This is their lot, and the Lord help them to fulfil their calling. These must for years to come be our active spirits: they are our strength and our hope. The fathers must soon go off the stage: their maturity in grace shows that they are ready for glory, and it is not God's way to keep his shocks of corn in the field when once they are fully ripe for the garner—perfect men shall be gathered up with the perfect, and shall enter into their proper sphere. The fathers, therefore, must soon be gone; and when they are gone, to whom are we to look for a succession but to these young men? We hope to have them for many years with us, valiant for the truth, steadfast in the faith, ripening in spirit, and growingly made meet to take their seats among the glorified saints above. Judge ye, dear brethren, whether ye are fairly to be ranked among the young men. Have no regard to the matter of sex, for there is neither male nor female in Christ Jesus. Judge whether ye be fit to be ranked among those whose full-grown and vigorous life entitles them to stand among the effectives of the church, the vigorous manhood of the seed of Israel. To such I speak. May God the Holy Spirit bless the word!

I. The first thing that John notes about these young men is THEIR POSSESSION OF STRENGTH:—"I have written unto you young men, because ye are strong."

These Christians of the middle class are emphatically strong. This does not imply that any measure of spiritual strength was in them by nature; for the Apostle Paul clearly puts it otherwise concerning our natural state saying, "When we were yet without strength, Christ died for the ungodly"; so that by nature we are without strength to do anything that is good and right. We are strong as a wild bull, to dash headlong into everything that is evil: strong as a lion to fight against all that is good and Godlike; but for all spiritual things and holy things we are utterly infirm and incapable; yea, we are as dead men until God the Holy Spirit deals with us.

Neither does the apostle here at all allude to the strength of the body in young men, for in a spiritual sense this is rather their weakness than their strength. The man who is strong in the flesh is too often for that very reason strongly tempted to sins of the flesh; and hence the apostle bids his young friend "flee youthful lusts." Whenever you read the life of Samson you may thank God you had not Samson's thews and sinews; or else it is more than probable that you would have had Samson's passions, and they might have mastered you as they mastered him. The time of life in which a young man is found is full of perils; and so is the spiritual condition of which it is the type. The young man might almost wish that it were with him as with the older man in whom the forces of the flesh have declined, for though age brings with it many infirmities it also has its gain in the abatement of the passions. So you see the young man cannot reckon upon vigour of the flesh as contributing towards real " strength ;" he has rather to ask for more strength from on high lest the animal vigour that is within him should drag down his spirit. He is glad to be in robust health that he may bear much toil in the Lord's cause ; but he is not proud of it, for he remembers that the Lord delighteth not in the strength of the horse, and taketh not pleasure in the legs of a man.

These young men in grace are strong, first of all, *in faith*, according to that exhortation, " Be strong ! fear not !" They have known the Lord now for some time, and they have enjoyed that perfect peace which comes of forgiven sin : they have marked the work of the Spirit within themselves, and they know that it is no delusion, but a divine change ; and now they not only believe in Christ, but they know that they believe in him. They know whom they have believed, and they are persuaded that he is able to keep that which they have committed to him. That faith which was once a healing touch has now become a satisfying embrace ; that enjoyment which was once a sip has now become a draught, quenching all thirst ; ay, and that which was once a draught has become an immersion into the river of God, which is full of water : they have plunged into the river of life and find waters to swim in. Oh what a mercy it is to be strong in this fashion. Let him that is strong take heed that he glory only in the Lord who is his righteousness and strength ; but in him and his strength he may indeed make his boast and defy the armies of the aliens. What saith Paul—"I can do all things through Christ that strengtheneth me." My brethren, take good heed that ye never lose this strength. Pray God that you may never sin so as to lose it ; may never backslide so as to lose it ; may never grieve the Spirit so as to lose it ; for I reckon that to be endowed with power from on High, and to be strong in faith, giving glory to God, is the truest glory and majesty of our manhood, and it were sad to lose it, or even to deface it. Oh that all Christians were so much advanced as to enter the enlisted battalion of the Lord's young men.

This strength makes a man strong *to endure.* He is a sufferer, but mark how patient he is ! He is a loser in business, and he has a hard task to earn his daily bread, but he never complains, he has learned in every state to be content. He is persecuted, but he is not distressed thereby : men revile him, but he is not moved from the even tenor of his way. He grows careless alike of flattery and calumny ; so long as he can please God he cares not to displease men. He dwells on high, and lives above the smoke of human opinion. He bears and forbears. He bows his neck to the yoke and his shoulders to the burden, and has fellowship with Christ in his sufferings. Blessed is that man who is so strong that he never complains of his trials, never whimpers and frets because he is made to share in the humiliations and griefs of his covenant head. He expected to bear the cross when he became a follower of the Crucified, and he is not now made weary and faint when it presses upon him. It is a fair sight to see young Isaac bearing the wood for the sacrifice : young Joseph bearing the fetters in prison with holy joy ;

young Samson carrying away the gates of Gaza, **bars** and all ; and young David praising God with his harp though Saul **is** feeling for his javelin. Such are the exploits of the young men who count it all joy when they fall into manifold trials for Christ's sake. O young man, be strong ; strong as an iron column which bears the full **stress** of the building and is not moved.

This strength shows itself, next, in *labouring for Christ.* The young man in Christ is a great worker. He has **so** much strength that he cannot sit still ; he would be ashamed to leave the burden and heat of the day to be borne by others. He is up and at it according to his calling and ability. He has asked his Lord as a favour to give him something to do. His prayer has been, "Show me what thou wouldst have me to do," and having received an answer he is found in the vineyard trenching the soil, removing the weeds, pruning the vines, and attending to such labours as the seasons demand. His Master has said to him, "Feed my sheep," and "Feed my lambs;" and, therefore, you shall see him through the livelong day and far into the night watching over the flock which is committed to him. In all this toil he greatly rejoices, for he is strong. He can run and not be weary ; he can walk and not faint. "By my God have I leaped over a wall," saith he. Nothing is hard to him ; or, if it be, he remembers that the diamond cuts the diamond, and so he sets a harder thing against a hard thing, and by a firm and stern resolution he overcomes. That which ought to be done he declares shall be done in the power of God, and lo, it is accomplished ! Blessed is the church that hath her quiver full of these ; she shall speak with her adversaries in the gate. These are the men that work our reformations ; these are the men who conduct our missions ; these are the men who launch out into the deep for Christ. They make the vanguard of the host of God, and largely compose the main body of her forces. I trust this church has many such. May they yet be multiplied and increased among us, that we may never lack for choice soldiers of the cross, able to lead on the hosts of God.

So, also, are these young men strong *to resist attack.* They are assaulted, but they carry with them the shield of faith wherewith they quench the fiery darts of the enemy. Wherever they go, if they meet with other tempted ones, they spring to the front to espouse their cause. They are ready in the day of battle to meet attacks upon the faith with the sword of the Spirit : they will yield no point of faith, but defend the truth at all hazards. Clad in the panoply of truth, they meet no deadly wound ; for by grace they are so preserved that the wicked one toucheth them not. They resist temptation, and are unharmed in the midst of peril. Do you want a specimen ? Look at Joseph ! Where ten thousand would have fallen he stands in snow-white purity. Joseph as contrasted with David is an instance of how a young man may bring greater glory to God than an older man when assailed by a kindred temptation. Joseph is but young, and the temptation forces itself upon him while he is in the path of duty. He is alone with his temptress, and no one need know of the sin if it be committed ; on the other hand, if he refuses, shame, and possibly death, may await him through the calumny of his offended mistress ; yet he bravely resists the assault, and overcomes the wicked one. He is a bright contrast to the older man, a father in Israel, who went out of his way to compass an evil deed, and committed crime in order to fulfil his foul desire. From this case we learn that neither years, nor knowledge, nor experience can preserve any one of us from sin ; but old and young must be kept by the power of God, or they will be overthrown by the tempter.

Furthermore, these young men are not only strong for resistance, but they are strong *for attack*. They carry the war into the enemy's territory. If there is anything to be done, they are like Jonathan and his armour-bearer, eager for the fray : these are very zealous for the Lord of hosts, and are prompt to undertake toil and travail for Jesus' sake. These smite down error, and set up truth : these believe great things, attempt great things, and expect great things, and the Lord is with them. The archers have sorely grieved them, and shot at them, and hated them ; but their bows abide in strength, for the arms of their hands are made strong by the mighty God of Jacob. One of them shall chase a thousand, and two put ten thousand to flight.

So have I shown you what these young men are : they are strong— strong to believe, strong to suffer, strong to do, strong to resist, strong to attack. May companies of these go in and out among us to fight the Lord's battles, for to this end hath the Lord girded them with strength.

II. Secondly, let us notice that he implies THEIR NEED OF STRENGTH ; for he says, " Ye are strong, and ye have overcome the wicked one." Between the lines of the text I read the fact, that young men who are strong must expect to be attacked. This also follows from a rule of divine economy. Whenever God lays up stores it is because there will be need of them. When Egypt's granaries were full with the supply of seven years of plenty, one might have been sure that seven years of famine were about to come. Whenever a man is strong it is because he has stern work to do ; for as the Israelite of old never had an ounce of manna left over till the morning except that which bred worms and stank, so there never will be a Christian that has a pennyworth of grace left over from his daily requirements. If thou art weak thou shalt have no trial happen to thee but such as is common to men ; but if thou be strong, rest thou assured that trials many and heavy are awaiting thee. Every sinew in the arm of faith will have to be tested. Every single weapon given out of the armoury of God will be called for in the conflict. Christian soldiering is no piece of military pastime ; it is no proud parade ; it means hard fighting from the day of enlistment to the day of reward. The strong young man may rest assured that he has no force to spend in display, no energy which he may use in vapouring and vainglory. There is a heavy burden for the strong shoulder, and a fierce fight for the trained hand.

Why does Satan attack this class of men most ? I reckon, first, because Satan is not always sure that the babes in grace are in grace, and therefore he does not always attack beginners ; but when they are sufficiently developed to make him see who and what they are, then he arouses his wrath. Those who have clean escaped from him he will weary and worry to the utmost of his power. A friend writes to me to enquire whether Satan knows our thoughts. Of course he does not, as God does. Satan pretty shrewdly guesses at them from our actions

and our words, and perhaps even from manifestations upon our counte-
nances ; but it is the Lord alone who knows the thoughts of men
immediately and by themselves. Satan is an old hand at studying
human nature : he has been near six thousand years watching and tempting men and women, and therefore he is full of cunning ; but yet he
is not omniscient, and therefore it may be that he thinks such and such
a person is so little in grace that perhaps he is not in grace at all ; so
he lets him alone : but as soon as ever it is certain that the man is
of the royal seed, then the devil is at him. I do not know whether our
Lord was ever tempted at Nazareth, while he was yet in his obscurity ;
but the moment he was baptized, and the Spirit of God came upon him,
he was taken into the wilderness to be tempted of the devil. If you
become an avowed servant of God do not think the conflict is over : it
is then that the battle begins. Straight from the waters of baptism, it
may be, you will have to go into such a wilderness and such a conflict
as you never knew before. Satan knows that young men in grace can
do his kingdom great harm, and therefore he would fain slay them early
in the day, as Pharaoh wished to kill all the male children in Israel.
My brethren, you are strong to overthrow his kingdom, and therefore
you need not marvel that he desires to overthrow you.

I think it is right that young men should endure hardness, for else
they might become proud. It is hard to hide pride from men. Full of
strength, full of courage, full of patience, full of zeal, such men are
ready enough to believe the wicked one when he whispers that they are
perfect; and therefore trial is sent to keep them out of that grievous
snare of the evil one. The devil is used by God as a householder might
employ a black, smutty scullion to clean his pots and kettles. The
devil tempts the saint, and thus the saint sees his inward depravity,
and is no longer able to boast. The devil thinks he is going to destroy
the man of God, but God is making the temptation work for the believer's
eternal good. Far better to have Beelzebub, the god of flies, pestering
you, than to become fly-blown with notions of your own excellence.

Besides, not only might this young man be a prey to pride, but he
certainly would not bring the glory to God untried that he brings to
him when he overcomes temptation. Read the story of Job up to the
time when he is tempted. Say you, " We have no story to read."
Just so, there was nothing worthy of record, only that his flocks and
herds continued to multiply, that another child was born, and so forth.
There is no history to a nation when everything goes well ; and it is so
with a believer. But when trial comes, and the man plays the man, and
is valiant for God against the arch-enemy, I hear a voice from heaven.
saying, " Write." Now you shall have history—history that will glorify
God. It is but right that those who are young men in Christ should
endure conflicts that they may bring honour to their Father, their
Redeemer, and the Holy Spirit who dwells in them.

Besides, it prepares them for future usefulness, and here I venture to
intrude the testimony of my own experience. I often wondered, when
I first came to Christ, why I had such a hard time of it when I was
coming to the Lord, and why I was so long and so wearied in finding a
Saviour. After that, I wondered why I experienced so many spiritual
conflicts while others were in peace. Ah, brethren, I did not know that

I was destined to preach to this great congregation. I did not understand in those days that I should have to minister to hundreds, and even thousands, of distressed spirits, storm-tossed, and ready to perish. But it is so now with me that when the afflicted mention their experience I can, as a rule, reply, "I have been there"; and so I can help them, as one who has felt the same. It is meet, therefore, that the young men should bear the yoke in their youth, and that while they are strong they should gain experience, not so much for themselves as for others, that in after days when they come to be fathers they may be able to help the little ones of the family. Take your tribulation kindly, brother: yea, take it gratefully; thank your King that he puts you in commission where the thick of the battle centres around you. You will never be a warrior if you never enter the dust-clouds where garments are rolled in blood. You will never become a veteran if you do not fight through the long campaign. The man who has been at the head of the forlorn hope is he who can tell what stern fighting means. So be it unto you: may your Captain save you from the canker of inglorious ease. You must fight in order that you may acquire the character which inspires others with confidence in you, and thus fits you to lead your comrades to the fray. Oh, that we may have here an abundance of the young men of the heavenly family who will defend the church against worldliness and error, defend the weaker ones from the wolves that prowl around, and guard the feeble against the many deceivers that waylay the church of God! As you love the Lord, I charge you grow in grace and be strong, for we have need of you just now. Oh, my brethren, take hold on sword and buckler; watch ye, and stand fast! May the Lord teach your hands to war and your fingers to fight. In these evil days may you be as a phalanx to protect our Israel. The Canaanites, the Hivites and the Jebusites are upon us just now; war is in all our borders: now, therefore, let each valiant man stand about the King's chariot, each man with his sword upon his thigh, because of fear in the night.

III. Thirdly, the text reminds us of THEIR PROOF OF STRENGTH: they have overcome the wicked one. Then they must be strong; for a man who can overcome the wicked one is no mean man of war—write him down among the first three. Wicked ones abound; but there is one crafty being who deserves the name of *the* wicked one: he is the arch-leader of rebellion, the first of sinners, the chief of sinners, the tempter of sinners. He is the wicked one who heads assaults against the pilgrims to Zion. If any man has ever stood foot to foot with him he will never forget it: it is a fight that once fought will leave its scars, even though the victory be won.

In what sense have these young men overcome the wicked one?

Well, first, in the fact that they have broken right away from his power. They were once his slaves, they are not so now. They once slept beneath his roof in perfect peace: but conscience raised an uproar, and the Spirit of God troubled them, and they clean escaped his power. Once Satan never troubled them at all. Why should he? They were good friends together. Now he tempts them and worries them, and assaults them because they have left his service, engaged themselves to a new master, and become the enemies of him who was once their god. I speak to many who gladly own that not a bit of them now belongs to the devil, from the crown of their head to the sole of their foot; for Christ has bought them, body, soul, and spirit, with his precious blood, and they have assented to the purchase, and feel that they are not their own, and certainly not the devil's; for they are bought with a price, and belong to him who purchased them. The strong man armed has been turned out by a stronger than he: Jesus has carried the fortress of the heart by storm, and driven out the foe. Satan is not inside our heart now; he entered into Judas, but he cannot enter into us; for our soul is filled by another who is well able to hold his own. The wicked one has been expelled by the Holy One, who now lives and reigns within our nature as Lord of all.

Moreover, these young men have overcome the wicked one, not only in breaking away from his power and in driving him entirely out of possession so that he is no longer master, but they have overcome him in the very fact of their opposition to him. When a man resists Satan, he is victorious over Satan in that very resistance. Satan's empire consists in the yielding of our will to his will; but when our will revolts against him, then already we have in a measure overcome him. Albeit that sometimes we are much better at willing than we are at doing, as the Apostle Paul was; for he said, "To will is present with me; but how to perform that which is good I find not"; yet, still, the hearty will to be clean from sin is a victory over sin; and as that will grows stronger and more determined to resist the temptations of the evil one, in that degree we have overcome sin and Satan. What a blessed thing this is! for fail not to remember that Satan has no weapons of defence, and so, when we resist him, he must flee. A Christian man has both defensive and offensive weapons, he has a shield as well as a sword: but Satan has fiery darts, and nothing else. I never read of his having any shield whatever: so that when we resist him he is bound to run away. He has no defence for himself, and the fact of our resistance is in itself a victory.

But, oh brothers and sisters, besides that, some of us who are young men in Christ have won many a victory over Satan. Have we not been tempted, fearfully tempted? But the mighty grace of God has come to the rescue, and we have not yielded. Cannot you look back, not with Pharisaic boasting, but with gracious exultation, over many an evil habit which once had the mastery over you, but which is master of you no longer? It was a hard conflict. How you bit your lip sometimes, and feared that you must yield! In certain moments your steps had almost gone, your feet had well-nigh slipped; but here you are conqueror yet! Thanks be to God who giveth us the victory through our Lord Jesus Christ. Hear what the Spirit saith to you when John writes to you: because you have overcome the wicked one, he says, "Love not the world, neither the things that are in the world."

Once more, in Christ Jesus we have entirely overcome the wicked one already; for the enemy we have to contend with is a vanquished foe— our Lord and Master met him and destroyed him. He is now destitute of his boasted battle-axe, that terrible weapon which has made the bravest men to quail when they have seen it in his hand. "What weapon is that?" say you. That weapon is death. Our Lord overthrew him that had the power of death, that is, the devil, and therefore

Satan has not the power of death any longer. The keys of death and of hell are at the girdle of Christ. Ah, fiend, we who believe in Jesus shall defeat thee, for our Lord defeated thee! That bruise upon thy head cannot be hidden! Thy crown is dashed in pieces! The Lord has sore wounded thee, O dragon, and never can thy deadly wound be healed! We have at thee with dauntless courage; for we believe the promise of our Lord, that he will bruise Satan under our feet shortly. As certainly as thou wast bruised under the feet of our crucified Lord, so shalt thou be bruised under the feet of all his seed, to thine utter overthrow and contempt. Let us take courage, brothers, and abide steadfast in the faith; for we have in our Lord Jesus overcome the wicked one. We are more than conquerors through him that hath loved us.

IV. Now I close with my fourth point, which is, THEIR SOURCE OF STRENGTH. You have seen their strength and their need of it, and their proof of it; now for the fountain of it. "The word of God abideth in you." I labour under the opinion that there never was a time in which the people of God had greater need to understand this passage than now. We have entered upon that part of the pilgrim path which is described by Bunyan as the Enchanted Ground : the church and the world appear to be alike bewitched with folly. Half the people of God hardly know their head from their heels at this time. They are gaping after wonders, running after a sounding brass and a tinkling cymbal, and waiting for yet more astounding inventions. Everything seems to be in a whirligig; a tornado has set in, and the storm is everywhere. Christians used to believe in Christ as their leader, and the Bible as their rule : but some of them are pleased with lords and rules such as he never knew! Believe me, there will soon come new Messiahs. Men are already pretending to work miracles, we shall soon have false Christs; and " Lo! here " and " Lo! there " will be heard on all sides. Anchors are up, winds are out, and the whole fleet is getting into confusion. Men in whose sanity and stability I once believed are being carried away with one fancy or another, and I am driven to cry, " What next? and what next? " We are only at the beginning of an era of mingled unbelief and fanaticism. Now we shall know who are God's elect and who are not; for there are spirits abroad at this hour that would, if it were possible, deceive even the very elect; and those who are not deceived are, nevertheless, sorely put to it. Here is the patience of the saints; let him look to himself who is not rooted and grounded in Christ, for the hurricane is coming. The signs of the times indicate a carnival of delusions; men have ceased to be guided by the word, and claim to be themselves prophets. Now we shall see what we shall see. Blessed is the sheep that knows his Shepherd, and will not listen to the voice of strangers. But here is the way to be kept steadfast—" The word of God abideth in you."

" *The word of God* "—that is to say, we are to believe in the doctrines of God's word, and these will make us strong. What vigour they infuse into a man! Get the word well into you, and you will overcome the wicked one. When the devil tempted Luther, the Reformer's grand grip of justification by faith made him readily victorious. Keep you a fast hold of the doctrines of grace and Satan will soon give over attacking you, for they are like plate-armour, through which no dart can ever force its way.

The promises of God's word, too, what power they give a man. To get a hold of a "shall" and "will" in the time of trouble is a heavenly safeguard. "My God will hear me." "I will not fail thee nor forsake thee." These are divine holdfasts. Oh, how strong a man is for overcoming the wicked one when he has such a promise to hand! Do not trust yourself out of a morning in the street till you have laid a promise under your tongue. I see people put respirators on in foggy weather; they do not make them look very lovely, but I dare say they are useful. I recommend the best respirator for the pestilential atmosphere of this present evil world when I bid you fit a promise to your lips. Did not the Lord rout the tempter in the wilderness with that promise, "Man shall not live by bread alone, but by every word that proceedeth out of the mouth of God shall man live"? Get the promises of God to lodge within you, and you will be strong.

Then mind the precepts, for a precept is often a sharp weapon against Satan. Remember how the Lord Jesus Christ struck Satan a killing blow by quoting a precept,—"It is written, Thou shalt worship the Lord thy God, and him only shalt thou serve." If the precept had not been handy, wherewith would the adversary have been rebuked? Nor is a threatening at all a weak weapon. The most terrible threatenings of God's word against sin are the best helps for Christians when they are tempted to sin:—How can I do this great wickedness, and sin against God? How should I escape if I turned away from him that speaketh from heaven? Tell Satan the threatenings, and make him tremble. Every word of God is life to holiness and death to sin. Use the word as your sword and shield: there is none like it.

Now notice that John not only mentions "the word of God," but the word of God "*in you*." The inspired word must be received into a willing mind. How? The Book which lies *there* is to be pleaded *here*, in the inmost heart, by the work of the Holy Ghost upon the mind. All of *this* letter has to be translated into spirit and life. "The word of God abideth in you"—that is, first to know it,—next to remember it and treasure it up in your heart. Following upon this, we must understand it, and learn the analogy of faith by comparing spiritual things with spiritual till we have learned the system of divine truth, and are able to set it forth and plead for it. It is, next, to have the word in your affections, to love it so that it is as honey or the droppings of the honeycomb to you. When this is the case you must and shall overcome the wicked one. A man instructed in the Scriptures is like an armed knight, who when he goes among the throng inflicts many a wound, but suffers none, for he is locked up in steel.

Yes, but that is not all; it is not the word of God in you alone, it is "the word of God *abideth* in you." It is always there, it cannot be removed from you. If a man gets the Bible right into him he is all right then, because he is full, and there is no room for evil. When you have filled a measure full of wheat you have effectually shut the chaff out. Men go after novel and false doctrines because they do not really know the truth; for if the truth had gotten into them and filled them, they would not have room for these day-dreams. A man who truly knows the doctrines of grace is never removed from them: I have heard our opponents rave at what they call the obstinacy of our brethren.

Once get the truth really into you, it will enter into the texture of your being, and nothing will get it out of you. It will also be your strength, by setting you watching against every evil thing. You will be on your guard if the word abides in you, for it is written, "When thou goest it will keep thee." The word of God will be to you a bulwark and a high tower, a castle of defence against the foe. Oh, see to it that the word of God is in you, in your very soul, permeating your thoughts, and so operating upon your outward life, that all may know you to be a true Bible-Christian, for they perceive it in your words and deeds.

This is the sort of army that we need in the church of God—men that are strong by feeding on God's word. Aspire to it, my brethren and sisters, and when you have reached it, then aspire unto the third degree that you may become fathers in Israel? Up to this measure, at any rate, let us endeavour to advance, and advance at once.

Are there any here who are not young men in Christ Jesus because they are not in Christ Jesus at all? I cannot speak with you this morning, for my time is gone; but I am distressed for you. To be out of Christ is such an awful thing that a man had better be out of existence. Without God, without Christ—then you are without joy in life or hope in death. Not even a babe in the divine family! Then know this, that God shall judge those that are without, and when he cometh how swift and overwhelming will that judgment be! Inasmuch as you would not have Christ in this day, Christ will not have you in that day. Stay not out of Christ any longer! Seek his face and live, for "he that believeth in him hath everlasting life." May you be enabled to believe in him at this moment, for Jesus' sake. Amen.

7 Supposing Him to Have Been in the Company

"Supposing him to have been in the company."—Luke ii. 44.

ALL who were present on the occasion are sure to remember our meditation upon, " Supposing him to be the gardener." Although it was only supposition, and evidently a mistake, yet it yielded us most profitable thought. Here is another supposition, a mistake again—a mistake which yielded a good deal of sorrow to those who made it; and yet in the hands of God's Spirit it may bring forth profitable instruction to us as we think it over.

I. We will begin our discourse by saying that THIS WAS A MOST NATURAL SUPPOSITION. That the child Jesus should have been in the company returning to Nazareth was a most likely thing. When the Jews came up from their different allotments once in the year to Jerusalem, they formed family groups at their first starting, and then as they got a little on the road these groups combined and made larger bands ; and as the roads approached to Jerusalem, the people gathered into great caravans : thus they went up to the House of God in company. It must have been a delightful season, especially if they sang those " Psalms of degrees " which are supposed to have been written for such pilgrims. What with prayer, and praise, and holy conversation, and with the prospect of meeting together in Jerusalem, the throne of the great King, they must have been happy bands of pilgrims. It was natural enough that, when all was over at Jerusalem, the child Jesus should return home : knowing the time when his parents would return, he would be ready to start with them, and failing to meet with them he would join the company with which he came, and so go back to Nazareth.

His parents did not expect to find him wandering alone: they looked for him in the company. Jesus was a child who loved society. He was not stoical, and thus selfishly self-contained ; and he was not sullen, avoiding society. He did not affect singularity. In the highest sense he was singular, for he was "holy, harmless, undefiled, separate from sinners"; but throughout his life he never aimed at singularity either

75

in dress, food, speech, or behaviour. He grew up to be a man among men, mixing with them even at weddings and funerals : no man was more truly human than the man Christ Jesus. It is to be believed that as a child he was like other children in all things but sin ; even as a man he was like other men in all but evil. Jesus was not one whose company would be shunned because of his ill manners ; rather would it be courted because of the sweetness of his disposition. He would not make himself disagreeable, and then crown that disagreeableness by stealing away from those whom he had vexed. They knew the sweetness of their dear child's character and the sociableness of his disposition, and there-fore they supposed him to have been in the company. This supposition would even more readily occur to us, knowing what we know about him, which is more than his parents knew ; for we know that of old his delights were with the sons of men, we know that he often came among men in angel form before his incarnation, and that when he came into the world he came seeking men. As a man he never seemed happier than when he was in the midst of his disciples, or surrounded by publicans and sinners, or feeding famishing crowds. He was so great a lover of mankind that he loved to be " in the company." Living and working in such a city as this, with all its millions, the burden is enough to break one's heart as we consider the city's sin, its irreligion, its neglect of God. It is sweet to hope that he who loved to be " in the company" when he was here, will certainly come and bless these throngs of men. If ever a physician was wanted, it is in this vast hospital ; if ever a shepherd was needed, it is among these perishing sheep. Jesus has such a love to the sons of men, and such a wish to gather them to himself, that even now his redeeming work is done he is still ever with us. He has been lifted up, and now he draws all men to himself ; and therefore do we expect to find him in the centre of these throngs. Those who go into the dense masses of humanity may expect this same Jesus to be with them in full power to save. Rescue the perishing, and he will be in the company. It was a most natural supposition, because of the sweetness and friendliness of his temper, that they would find Jesus in the company.

They never suspected that he would be found in any wrong place. No thought ever crossed their minds that he would be found in any haunt of vice, or in any assembly of vanity, though such could have been found in Jerusalem. We *do* expect to meet our Lord amid the throng of perishing men and women, seeking and saving them ; but we know that we shall not find him among those who find pleasure in noisy laughter and lawless mirth. We never look for Jesus in the theatre or the drinking saloon : it would be profanity to suppose him there. We never look for him where a question of morals might be raised, for he is un-defiled. We expect to find him where his people meet for worship ; we look for him where honest men are labouring hard for their daily bread, or where they lie suffering his Father's will ; but we never dream of his being found where the world, the flesh, and the devil hold supreme control. Let his example be followed by us : let us never go where our Master would not have gone. There are some places where we cannot suppose him to have been ; in those places let it not be supposable that we can be. Let us go only where we can remain in fellowship with our divine Master, and where we should be happy to be found if he were suddenly to come in his kingdom. Let us judge of where we may go by enquiring, "Would Jesus have gone there?" and if he would not have gone, let our feet refuse to carry us that way.

II. But, secondly, THIS SUPPOSITION BROUGHT THEM GREAT SORROW ; from which I gather that we ought, with regard to the Lord Jesus Christ, to leave nothing as a matter of supposition. By supposing him to have been in the company, they were made to miss him, and to seek him sorrowing for three days. Why did they lose sight of him at all? Why did they not abide with him? We may not blame them, for *he* did not : but, at any rate, they fell into days and nights of trouble by supposing something about him. Do not suppose anything about Jesus at all. Do not suppose anything about his character, his doctrine, or his work; go in for certainty on such points. I have heard of a German who evolved a camel out of his own inner consciousness; what kind of a camel it was I do not know : but many persons evolve a Christ out of their own imaginations. Do not so; for if you do this you will make to yourselves a Christ nothing like Jesus; it will be a mere image, a false Christ, an idol Christ. No human thought could ever have invented our Saviour. We put it to all those who doubt the inspiration of the four evangelists—would they kindly write us a fifth evangel? Would they even suggest another action of Jesus which would fit into the rest and be of the same order? They cannot do it. The whole conception of Jesus is original and divine. It is not possible that the most ingenious fancy can add anything to the life of Christ which would square with that which is recorded. If you chance to read the *Prot-evangelion*, or *the Gospel of the Infancy*, which are spurious narratives of the childhood of Jesus, you will throw them into the fire and say at once, "These do not fit in with the records of the true evangelists : these stories are ludicrously unlike the child Jesus." In fact, all the books which pretend to be a part of the canon will be detected and rejected at once by the simplest reader who is thoroughly versed in the four evangelists. Do not, therefore, *suppose* anything concerning Jesus, but read the word of God and see what is revealed about him. Never clip the King's coin, but accept it as it is minted in all its purity and preciousness. Add not to the perfect word, lest plagues be added to you. What the Holy Ghost has written concerning the man Christ Jesus, the everlasting Son of God, receive humbly, but do not import suppositions into your theology. This has been the cause of the division of the church into sects : the bones of contention have not been truths revealed, but fictions imagined. I may invent one theory, and another man another, and we shall each fight for his theory. An hypothesis is set up and supported by the letter of Scripture, though not by the spirit of it; and straightway men begin to differ, dispute, and divide. Let us lay aside all suppositions, for these things will only bring us sorrow in the end. Let us believe in the real Jesus as he is revealed in the Scriptures, and as the Holy Ghost graciously enables us to behold him in the glass of the word.

"Supposing him to have been in the company." This supposition caused them great sorrow. Again, I say, beloved, do not take anything about Jesus at haphazard and peradventure. Let this truth apply to your personal dealing with him; as, for instance, do not suppose him to be *in your hearts.* Do not suppose that because you were baptized in infancy you are therefore in Christ and Christ in you. That is a dangerous supposition. Do not say, "But I have been baptized as a professed believer, and therefore Jesus is in my heart." The inward grace is not tied to the outward sign. Water baptism does not convey the Spirit of God. Blessed are they who, having the Spirit, can use the ordinance to their profit; but do not suppose that the grace of God is tied to any outward rite. Do not say, "I have eaten at the communion table, and therefore Jesus is in my heart." You may eat and drink at his table, and yet never know him, and he may never know you. Outward ceremonies convey no grace to graceless persons. Do not take it for granted that because you are admitted into a Christian church, and are generally accepted as being a believer, that therefore you must needs be so. I dread lest any of you should think your church membership to be a certificate of salvation. It was not given to you with that view; we judged favourably of your conduct and profession, but we could not read your heart. Do not even suppose that grace must necessarily be in your souls because you have been professing Christians for a great many years, for the lapse of time will not turn falsehood into truth. It is difficult to know how long hypocrisy can be kept up, or how far a man may be self-deceived; it is even possible that he may die with his eyes blinded through the exceeding deceitfulness of sin. Do not suppose that Jesus is in your heart because you are an elder, or a deacon, or a pastor. I will not make any supposition in my own case, for woe is unto me if, after having preached to others, I myself should be a castaway! Such things have happened: Judas was one of the twelve. Men have been sweet of voice, and yet bitter of heart: they have been taught in the word of God as to the letter thereof, but they have not known the power of the everlasting Spirit, and so they have perished. Verily, I say unto you, in Christ's name, unless the Spirit of God do actually rest upon each one of us personally, it will be all in vain for us to suppose that he is in our hearts because of professions and ordinances, for the supposition may be a damning falsehood, and may lull us into a fatal slumber. How terrible to be taken out to execution with our eyes bandaged by a supposition!

Again, dear friends, do not ever *suppose* that Christ is *in our assemblies* because we meet in this house. Do not go up to a place of worship and say Jesus is sure to be there. He may not have been there for many a day. Is it not sad that out of the tens of thousands of assemblies held on this day there will be many in which Jesus will not be present; for his gospel will not be preached, or if preached, it will not be set forth in the living power of the Holy Ghost? Christ is not present where he is not honoured. All your architecture, all your millinery, all your music, all your learning, all your eloquence are of small account; Jesus may be absent when all these things are present in profusion; and then your public worship will only be the magnificent funeral of religion, but the life of God will be far away. It brings great sorrow in the long run to a church if they take it for granted that Jesus must be among them. Our question every Sunday morning ought to be, "What think ye, will *he* come to the feast?" for if he does not come to the feast it will be the mockery of a festival, but no bread will be on the table for hungry souls. We must have our Lord in our company or we will break our hearts over his absence. We desire his presence even in the smallest prayer-meeting, and in our minor gatherings when we meet to consult as to his work. If he arouses us by his Spirit, and discovers to us that he was not in our former meetings, we will seek him sorrowing, as his father and mother did.

Once more, let us not take it for granted that the Lord Jesus is necessarily with us *in our Christian labours*. Do we not too often go out to do good without special prayer, imagining that Jesus must surely be with us as a matter of course? Perhaps we thus conclude because he has been with us so long, or because we feel ourselves fully equipped for the occasion, or because we do not even think whether he is with us or not. This is perilous. If Jesus is not with us, we toil all the night and we take nothing; but if Jesus is with us, he teaches us how to cast the net, and a great multitude of fishes are taken. If Jesus be not with us, we are like Samson when his hair was shorn: he went out as at other times thinking to smite the Philistines hip and thigh, as he had done before, but as Watts puts it, he—

> "Shook his vain limbs with vast surprise,
> Made feeble fight, and lost his eyes."

So shall we be defeated if we imagine that we can now succeed without fresh divine assistance; the fact being that we ought to seek the Lord in prayer before the smallest Christian engagement, and then we may reap in it the most important result of our lives. You are going to see a poor bedridden old woman; do not attempt to comfort this king's daughter without first seeking the presence of "the Consolation of Israel." You are going to teach your Sunday-school class this afternoon; you have taken it so many times that you get your dinner and walk off to the school scarcely thinking enough about what you are doing to breathe a prayer for your Lord's help? Is this right? Can you afford to waste one single Sabbath afternoon, or one opportunity to speak for Jesus? and yet it will be wasted if he be not with you. Some of your children may be dead before next Sunday, or never come to the class again; go not even once without your Lord. Do not sit down to teach as if you had Jesus at your command, and were sure that of necessity he must succeed your endeavours. He will withdraw from us if we fall into a careless, prayerless habit. Why was he not with his mother that day? Truly he had to be about the business of his heavenly Father, but why did he permit his human mother to miss him? Was it not because she needed to be taught, as well as the rest of us, the value of his company. Perhaps, if we never missed him, we might not know how sweet he is. I can picture Mary, when she had lost the dear child, weeping floods of tears. Then she began to understand what old Simeon meant when he said, "Yea, a sword shall pierce through thine own heart also." The sword was piercing her heart even then to prepare her for three other days in which she would mourn him as dead with still bitterer grief. See how she enquired everywhere, "Have ye seen him?" She reminds me of the spouse in the Song, "Saw ye him whom my soul loveth?" I think I see her going through the streets, and saying at the close of the day, " I sought him, but I found him not." Everywhere the same question, " Saw ye him whom my soul loveth ? " but she gets no tidings of him. Peace is all unknown to her till she finds him. But, oh, how precious he was in her eyes when at last she discovered him in the temple. How careful she was of him afterwards, how happy to think that no harm had come to her dear charge! If you and I ever lose the society of Christ in our service we will go to him, and cry, " My Lord, do not leave me again. What a fool I am if thou art not my wisdom! How weak I am if thou art not my strength! How worse than silent I am if thou art not mouth to me! How heartless is all my talk, and how flat it falls upon the hearers' ears, if thou art not the spirit and the life of all my speaking!" Oh, if all our preaching and teaching were in the power of the presence of our divine Master, how different it would be!

Do, then, learn the lesson, brethren, as I desire to learn it for myself, that we must not take anything for granted about Jesus. We must make sure work concerning eternal things, for if these be allowed to slip, where are we? Grasp the truth, and know that it is the truth. Never be satisfied with " ifs," and " buts," and " I hope so," and " I trust so," but make sure of Christ! If you are not sure about the health of your body, yet be sure about your being in Christ, and so healthy in soul. If you are not sure about the solvency of your firm, if you are not sure about the deeds of your estate, if you are not sure about your marriage lines, yet at least be sure that you have Jesus within your heart. If you have any doubt to-day, give no sleep to your eyes nor slumber to your eyelids until the Holy Ghost himself hath sealed upon your spirit the certainty that Jesus is yours. Thus have I used the supposition in two ways.

III.   Now for a third lesson : THE SUPPOSITION made by these two good people MAY INSTRUCT US. Let us use it at this time, and turn to " Supposing him to have been in the company."

I speak now to children who are hearing this sermon. This is for you. Jesus was about twelve years old, and you are of much the same age. Suppose he had been in the company returning to Nazareth. How would he have behaved himself? Think of Jesus as an example for yourselves. I am sure when the whole company sang a psalm that bright-eyed boy *would have been among the sweetest singers:* he would have sung most heartily the praises of God his Father. There would have been no inattention or weariness in him when God was to be praised. Among the most devout worshippers you would number the holy child. Therefore, dear children, whenever you come in among God's people, give your whole hearts to the worship: pray with us and sing with us, and endeavour to drink in the truth which is spoken, for so will you be like the holy Jesus. Let all boys and girls pray that among God's people they may behave as Jesus would have done.

I feel persuaded that Jesus would have been found in that company *listening to those who talked of holy things;* especially would he have been eager to hear explanations of what he had seen in the temple. When the conversation turned upon the Paschal lamb, how that dear child, who was also "the Lamb of God, which taketh away the sin of the world," would have listened to it! I think I see his sweet face turned towards those who spoke of the sprinkled blood. He would surely have said, "What mean ye by this ordinance?" He would have been anxious to share with the grown-up people all the solemn thoughts of the day. So whenever you come up to the house of God try and learn all that you can from all the teaching of God's word. Seek good company, and learn by it. Have a deaf ear to those who speak wickedly, but always be ready to listen to everything about your God, your Saviour, your faith, and the heaven where you hope to dwell.

I feel sure also that if he had been in the company going home *he would have been the most obliging, helpful, pleasing child* in all the company: if anybody had needed to have a burden carried, this boy of twelve would have been the first to offer, as far as his strength allowed; if any kindly deed could be done, he would be first in doing it. He grew in favour both with God and men because he laid himself out to be everybody's servant. Mary's son won the love of all around, for he was so unselfish, kind, gentle, and willing. He did all that he could to make others happy; and blessed are those boys and girls who learn this lesson well. Oh, children, you will be happy yourselves if you live to make others happy! Act thus to your parents, brothers and sisters, friends and schoolfellows, and you will in this be like Jesus.

I am sure, also, that Jesus would not have done in that company as too many boys are apt to do. *He would not have been mischievous, noisy, annoying, and disobedient;* but he would have been a comfort and delight to all about him. No doubt but he would have been the liveliest and most cheerful boy in the whole company, but yet he would not have been rough, coarse, wilful, or cruel. There would have been no quarrelling where he was; his very presence would have bred peace amongst all the children that were with him. I should like you to think over all that Jesus would have done and would not have done, and then I should be glad to see you acting as he did. Take this little word home with you, dear children,—Ask yourselves often, *what would Jesus do?* for what Jesus would have done is the best rule for you.

And now to you elder folks, "supposing him to have been in the company," and you had been in the company, I will warrant there is not one father or mother but what *would have been willing to care for him*. Every matron here says, "I would have taken him under my wing." You say that honestly, do you not? You mean it, I am sure. Well, you have an opportunity of proving that you are sincere; for Jesus is still in our company. You can find him in the form of the poor. If you would have watched over *him*, relieve their wants; do it to the least of these, and you have done it unto him. You can find Jesus in the form of the sick; visit them. I wish more of God's people would addict themselves to calling upon the sick, visiting them in their loneliness, and cheering them in their needs. As you say you would have taken care of Jesus, prove it at once by remembering his words, "I was sick, and ye visited me." If you would have taken care of Jesus, you can show it by caring for the young, for every young child comes to us under the guardian care of him who said, "Suffer the little children to come unto me, and forbid them not." You that spend your leisure in seeking to bless the young are proving that, if you had been in that company, you would have taken care of the child Jesus. Above all, consider the orphans; for, had he been in that company, he would have been practically an orphan, for he would have lost for a while both father and mother. Many among you have such fond maternal hearts that you would have said, " I must look after that bright, beautiful boy who is now without parents. Evidently he has lost them. Come here, child, come here!" You would have felt a joy to have kissed him, and folded him to your bosom. Prove it by looking after orphan children wherever they are, and let each represent to you the Jesus of that day as he would have been had his parents' supposition been correct. Let us see that the love you feel to Jesus when you read your Bibles is not mere emotion or sentiment, but that practical principle lies at the back of it, and this day affects your life and conduct. So far have we gone, and I hope not altogether without profit. May the Spirit of God help us yet further.

IV. But now I change the line of our thought altogether for a little while. Forget the child Jesus now, and let me use the words concerning Jesus in the fulness of his power. SUPPOSING HIM TO BE IN OUR COMPANY IN ALL HIS GRACIOUS INFLUENCE, what then ? Then, brethren, first, *how happy* will such company be ! For with Christ known to be in their company saints cannot but be glad. You may have seen a picture representing certain of the martyrs sitting in prison together. They are to be burned by-and-by, and they are comforting each other. Now, supposing him to have been in their company, as I doubt not he was, I could wish to have been there even at the price of sharing their burning —would not you ? Or see, a few poor people met together in a cottage talking about Jesus, as people seldom do now ; Jesus is there, and their hearts are burning within them! How favoured they are! If their hearts might otherwise have been sad, yet supposing him to be in the company, how restful all the mourners become; how light every burden grows, how every aching heart rejoices, for in his presence there is fulness of joy. Get but Christ into your family circle and it is a ring of delight.

Supposing Jesus to be in the company next *how united* his people will all become! Whenever Christian people fall out, it is because Jesus is not in the company. Whenever there is a lack of love, whenever there is a lack of forbearance, when people fall to fault-finding and quarrelling one with the other, my heart says to me, " Supposing him to have been in the company, they would not have acted so." They would have looked at *him*, and straightway have forgiven one another. Nay, they would hardly have had need to forgive, for they would neither have given nor taken offence, but their hearts would have flowed together in one common stream. The sheep are scattered everywhere upon the hills till the shepherd comes, but they know his voice, and they gather to his person. Jesus is the centre and the source of unity, and when we have him reigning in his full glory in the midst of the church divisions and schisms will cease to be.

" Supposing him to have been in the company," how *holy* they would all grow. Sin dies as Jesus looks upon it, and men's wayward passions yield to his sweet sway. How *devout* would all hearts be "supposing him to be in the company!" What prayer there is, and what praise! There is no hurrying over morning devotion, no falling asleep at the bedside at night when Jesus is in our company. Then our heart is praying all day long, and we delight to pray together for his coming and his kingdom.

How *teachable* we are, too, when Jesus is in the company, opening the Scriptures and opening our hearts; and what sweet *communion* we enjoy. How souls go out to his soul, and hearts to his heart, and how are we knit together in the one Christ! How happy, how united, how holy is the company supposing Jesus to be in it.

When Jesus is in the company how *lively* they all are. Why, in these warm mornings some seem half inclined to fall asleep, even in the house of prayer—"The spirit truly is willing, but the flesh is weak." But when Jesus is in the company the spirit triumphs over the flesh, and we feel full of life, and power, and energy in the divine service. When our hearts burn within us because of his words our bodies cannot freeze. When the soul is quickened by his presence, then the whole man is aroused. As when the sun rises his light wakes thousands of sleepers, though no voice is heard, so the smiles of Jesus arouse a sleeping church, and stir it to zeal and energy.

If Jesus be in the company, how *earnest* we grow! How zealous for his glory! How intent to win souls! I am afraid it is because Jesus is not in the company that we allow many sinners to go by us without a warning, and we neglect fine opportunities for serving our Lord. You have heard of holy Mr. Payson, the American divine, a man who walked with God in his ministry. He was out one day with a brother minister who had to make a call at a lady's house, and Payson went in with him. The lady pressed them both to stay to tea. She was not a Christian woman, and Payson had other business, and therefore he demurred; but as she pressed him very earnestly he sat down, and invoked the divine blessing, which he did in terms so sweet and full of holy unction that he impressed everybody. The lady waited upon him with great attention, and when he rose up to go he said to her, "Madam, I thank you much for your great kindness to me; but how do you treat my Master?" A work of grace was wrought in that lady by the question; she was brought to Jesus; she opened her house for preaching, and a revival followed. Now, if Jesus had not been with Payson, what had become of that woman? I fear that we go in and out among dying men and women, and we let them perish—yes, we let them be damned without an effort for their salvation, and all because we have not obeyed the voice which speaks to us as it did to Abraham, "I am God Almighty, walk before me, and be thou perfect." We shall never be perfected as the servants of God except we walk in his conscious presence; but if we walk before him, and he is with us, then shall we be earnest in the winning of souls.

I am sure, dear friends, that if Jesus be in the company then we shall be *confident*, and all doubts will vanish. How firmly shall we believe because we are living in fellowship with "the Truth"! How *safely* we shall be guarded against temptation, even as the sheep are safe from the wolf when the shepherd is near! What blessed, heavenly lives shall we lead! Surely, it will be small change for us to rise from earth to heaven if Jesus be always in the company, in the family, and in the business; in our labours and recreations, in our joys and sorrows.

V. Lastly, I want to dwell, for just a minute, by way of touching the conscience, upon the reflection that JESUS HAS BEEN IN THE COM-PANY, whether we have seen him or not. I want you now to look back upon what he has seen in your company, supposing him to have been there, when you were disputing the other night. Yes, a point of doctrine had come up, and you differed over it. Did you not wax very warm, my brother, even so as to grow red in the face? Did you not go away from that friend with whom you disputed almost hating him? You know you did. Supposing Jesus to have been in the company, he did not smile on that dispute. He was there, and he was grieved at the way in which you remembered his doctrine but forgot his spirit. Had you perceived his presence you would have put your argument much more sweetly, and you would have spoken, not for the sake of beating your friend in argument, but for the sake of instructing him and glorifying your Lord. You know that you did not yield a point you ought to have yielded; you knew you were wrong at the time, but your friend pushed you hard, and you said to yourself, "I will not give way, though I feel that he is right." Although I suppose that we shall differ about many points till the Lord comes, yet when differences arise they will present fair opportunities for holy charity and mutual edification, and these will gladly be seized if Jesus be in the company. When next we argue let each one say, "Jesus is in this company; therefore, while we speak up for what we believe to be true, let us do it in a loving spirit." Our arguments will not lose force by being steeped in love. Truth is never stronger than when it walks with charity.

Then, again, it may be that some little time ago certain of you were acting in such a way that no common observer could have seen any difference between you and worldlings. You were out in business, dealing with one who was trying to do his best for himself, and you were trying to do your best for yourselves. Do I blame you? Not for being prudent and circumspect; but I hope you will blame yourselves for going far beyond this. You did nothing which I may style dis-honest—but did you not sail dreadfully near the wind? You stated something which I must not call a lie, but still it was not true as you meant it to be understood: was it? Business men too often aim at getting undue advantage of each other: it is "diamond cut diamond," and rather worse at times. If Christian men in all their dealings would suppose Jesus to be in the company, how it would change their manners. Think of Jesus on this side the counter along with you who sell, and on that side of the counter along with you who buy. You both need his presence, for the buyer is generally quite as intent upon cheating as the seller; he wants the goods for less than they are worth, and the seller therefore baits the hook for him. Trade is growing rotten right through, but the blame is not all on one side. When persons must have goods far below the price for which they can be produced, they must not marvel if they find that they are sold an inferior article which looks well enough, but turns out to be worthless. Oh, that you Christian people would always suppose Jesus to be in your company. I can hardly imagine Judas cheating John with Jesus looking on; nor Philip trading hardly with the lad who had the barley loaves. Should not our dealings among the sons of men be such as Jesus can approve? He is our Master and Lord; let us imitate him, and do nothing that we shall be ashamed for him to look upon.

Do not accuse me of being personal this morning, for if you do, I will plead guilty. If the cap fits, you wear it. The other day you were in company, and certain persons were talking profanely, or was it scepticism which they vented? And you, as Christ's disciple, heard them, and what did you do? Did you bear witness for the truth? They made a joke—it was not over clean, but you laughed! Did you not? But, alas, you said nothing for your Lord! Yet he was in the company, seeing all! You had several opportunities, but you did not put in a word for truth and holiness. Now, supposing Jesus to have been in the company, I think he must have been sorely grieved. Surely your Lord must have thought, "What! all this said against me, and never a word in reply from him whom I redeemed with my own blood!" Was not this Peter over again in his denials of his Lord? You did not deny him with oaths and cursing, but the same cowardly spirit ruled you. Oh, if you had but come out in your true colours! You do not know what an influence you might have had for good. If we set the Lord Jesus Christ always before us, should we not be brave to testify and quick to defend?

Think, again, of those evenings when a few friends meet together: are they not often a waste of time? "Supposing him to have been in the company," as he really is, do you think the evenings should be spent as they frequently are? Dr. Chalmers, a truly devout man, tells us that once at a nobleman's house he spent an evening with various friends, and talked over the question of the cause and cure of pauperism—a subject most suitable for conversation. An aged Highland chieftain among the company listened with great attention to the Doctor, for Chalmers was master of the subject. Surely they had not spent the evening amiss: but in the night an unusual noise was heard, and a heavy groan. The chieftain was dying. In a few minutes he was dead, and Dr. Chalmers stood over him, the picture of distress. "Alas," he cried, "had I known that my friend was within a few minutes of eternity I would have preached to him and to you Christ Jesus and him crucified." With how much more reason may many Christians repent of their conversation! How bitterly may they look back upon wasted hours! Supposing Jesus to have been in the company, how often must he have been grieved by our frivolities! Do you not think that it is greatly to our discredit as Christian people that we should so often meet and so seldom pray? The happiest evenings that Christians spend are when they talk even upon secular subjects in a gracious manner, and do not fail to rise to holier themes, and mingle prayer and thanksgiving with their talk. Then when they retire they feel that they have spent the evening as Jesus would approve.

Did I not hear the other day of some Christian friend who was going to give up working for Christ? and of a dozen Christian friends who were going to break up, and no more go on with their holy service for Jesus? One was going to leave the Sunday-school in which he had been for years; another was going to allow a weak church to break up and go to pieces, for he had grown tired of working under discouragements: another said, "I have had my turn, let somebody else do the work now." Supposing Jesus to have been in the company, do you think that such observations pleased him? If Jesus were perceived among us, would any one of us turn his back in the day of battle? No, brethren, since Jesus is with us, let us serve him as long as we have any being. Recollect John Newton's speech when they told him that he was too old to preach: the venerable man exclaimed, "What, should the old African blasphemer cease to preach while there is breath in his body? Never!" Do not suffer any difficulty, or infirmity, to prevent your persevering in the service of Jesus in some form or other, and when you do feel as if you must leave the ranks, suppose him to be in the company, and march on! Forward, brethren! Jesus leads the way! Forward, for his presence is victory! God bless you, dear friends, and all this day may Jesus be in the company to make it a hallowed Sabbath to your souls. Amen.

8 The Exeter-Hall Sermon to Young People

"O Lord, truly I am thy servant; I am thy servant, and the son of thine handmaid: thou hast loosed my bonds."—Psalm cxvi. 16.

I HAVE been wondering whether I might correctly say that I would preach to-night as a young man to young men. It is precisely what I should like to do, but can I do it? You are young men, I see, to a very large extent; but I wonder whether I am a young man myself. I have two opinions upon it in my own mind. Sometimes I feel very old. When I look in the glass and see the hairs that have turned white upon my head, I suspect that I cannot be a young man; when I feel weary with my work and worn with sickness, I am persuaded that years are telling upon me; yet when I recover from sickness I feel young again, and when cheerful spirits and vivacity return I half hope that I may still be a young man. I must not, however, deceive myself, for when I come to calculate and tally all up, I confess that if youth be essential to membership with the Young Men's Christian Association I could not expect to be voted in. I am a little under fifty, and I am a grandfather; and so I do not think that I can call myself a young man. Very well; I will not take upon myself airs, and pretend to be what I am not, nor will I affect to be quite in your position upon the life-chart. I am not old, however. I suppose that I am just in the middle passage, and, as a man in the centre of life, I may venture to-night to give some little instruction and advice to you who are at its beginning. I have received a lot of advice myself in former years, and have borne it pretty patiently. Everybody has advised me. I must honestly own that I have not followed all their advice, or else I had not been here. But now I think that I shall take my turn, and see whether I may not give a little advice; and the advice, such as it is, shall come out of my own experience. I do not expect you blindly to follow it, for I have confessed that I have not always accepted everybody's counsel myself. Only give me a hearing: gather the good of what I say into vessels, and throw the bad away. Before I get quite away from being a young man I will try to talk with those who so lately were my comrades: before I shake hands with the old men, and ask for a seat among them, I would have a word with those who are coming upon the scene of action to fill our places.

I may say honestly at the very beginning that I want so to preach to-night that every man here who is not yet a servant of the Lord may at least desire to become one, and that very many may actually enlist in the service of our great Lord and Master on this very spot. Why not? I shall be thrice happy, and they will be thrice happy too, if such should be the case. Hence I have taken a text which I can repeat on my own behalf as sincerely as the Psalmist could for himself: "O Lord, truly I am thy servant; I am thy servant, and the son of thine handmaid: thou hast loosed my bonds."

I. I begin, then, dear young men, by COMMENDING THE SERVICE OF GOD TO YOU. I want you to enter it, and therefore I commend it.

When a young man starts in life he is apt to enquire of an older person in this fashion—"I should like to get into such a business, but is it a good one; you have been in it for years, how do you find it?" He seeks the advice of a friend who will tell him all about it. Some will have to warn him that their trade is decaying, and that there is nothing to be done in it. Others will say that their business is very trying, and that if they could get out of it they would; while another will answer for his work, "Well, I have found it all right. I must speak well of the bridge which has carried me over. I have been able to earn a living, and I recommend you to try it." I come here at this time on purpose to give my own experience, and therefore *I wish to say concerning the service of the Lord that I have never regretted that I entered it.* Surely, at some time or other, in these thirty-three years since I put on Christ's livery and became his servant, I should have found out the evil if there had been anything wrong in the religion of Jesus. At some time or other I should have discovered that there was a mistake, and that I was under a delusion. But it has never been so. I have regretted many things which I have done, but I have never regretted that I gave my heart to Christ and became a servant of the Lord. In times of deep depression—and I have had plenty of them—I have feared this and feared the other, but I have never had any suspicion of the goodness of my Master, the truth of his teaching, or the excellence of his service: neither have I wished to go back to the service of Satan and sin. Mark you, if we had been mindful of the country from whence we came out, we have had many an opportunity to return. All sorts of enticement have assailed me, and siren voices have often tried to lure me upon the rocks; but never, never since the day in which I enlisted in Christ's service have I said to myself, "I am sorry that I am a Christian; I am vexed that I serve the Lord." I think that I may, therefore, honestly, heartily, and experimentally recommend to you the service which I have found so good. I have been a bad enough servant, but never had a servant so lovable a Master or so blessed a service.

There is one thing, too, which will convince you that in my judgment the service of God is most desirable: *I have great delight in seeing my children in the same service.* When a man finds that a business is a bad one, you will not find him bringing up his boys to it. Now, the greatest desire of my heart for my sons was, that they might become the servants of God. I never wished for them that they might be great or rich, but, oh, if they would but give their young hearts to Jesus! This I prayed for most heartily. It was one of the happiest nights of my life when I baptized them into the name of the Father, and of the Son, and of the Holy Ghost, upon profession of their faith; and now, while I am speaking to you, one is preaching in New Zealand, and another at Greenwich; and my heart is glad that the gospel which the father preaches, the sons are preaching too. If my Lord's service had been a hard one, I should have said to these lads, "Don't you take to it. God is a hard Master, reaping where he has not strawed: I went into the service blindly, but I warn you to avoid it." My conduct has been the reverse of this, and thus I have given you hostages in the persons of my sons for my honest love to my Master and Lord: I do without reserve commend to you the service of the Lord Jesus Christ; for if you enter it, you will wish your sons and daughters to enter it; and it will be your ambition that to the latest generation all your house may fear and serve God.

I would add this more of personal testimony: so blessed is the service of God, that *I would like to die in it!* When I have been unable to preach through physical pain, I have taken my pen to write, and found much joy in making books for Jesus; and when my hand has been unable to wield the pen, I have wanted to talk about my Master to somebody or other, and I have tried to do so. I remember that David Brainerd, when he was very ill, and could not preach to the Indians, was found sitting up in bed, teaching a little Indian boy his letters, that he might read the Bible; and so he said, "If I cannot serve God one way, I will another. I will never leave off this blessed service." This is my personal resolve, and verily, there is no merit in it, for my Lord's service is a delight. It is a great pleasure to have anything to do for our great Father and Friend, and most affectionately, for your own good, I commend the service of God to you.

I think of it now in the following lights, and therefore I commend it to you for four reasons:

To serve God is the most reasonable thing in the world. It was he that made you: should not your Creator have your service? It is he that supports you in being: should not that being be spent to his glory? Oh, sirs, if you had a cow or a dog, how long would you keep either of them if it were of no service to you? Suppose it were a dog, and it never fawned upon you, but followed at everybody else's heel, and never took notice of *you*—never acknowledged *you* as its master at all: would you not soon tire of such a creature? Which of you would make an engine, or devise any piece of machinery, if you did not hope that it would be of some service to you? Now, God has made you, and a wonderful piece of mechanism is the body, and a wondrous thing is the soul; and will you never obey him with the body or think of him with the mind? This is Jehovah's own lament: "Hear, O heavens, and give ear, O earth: for the Lord hath spoken, I have nourished and brought up children, and they have rebelled against me. The ox knoweth his owner, and the ass his master's crib: but Israel doth not know, my people doth not consider." To have lived to be one-and-twenty without God is a terrible robbery; how have you managed it? To have lived to be thirty or forty, and never to have paid any reverence to him who has kept the breath in your nostrils, without which you would have been a loathsome carcase in the grave long ago, is a base injustice; how dare you continue in it? To have lived so long, and, in addition to that, to have often insulted God; to have spoken against him; to have profaned his day; to have neglected his Book; to have turned your back on the Son of his love—is not this enough? Will you not cease from such an evil course? Why, there are some men who cannot bear five minutes' provocation, nay, nor five seconds' either. It is "a word and a blow" with them; only the blow frequently comes first. But here is God provoked by the twenty years at a stretch—the thirty, the forty, the fifty years right on; and yet he bears patiently with us. Is it not time that we render to him our reasonable service? If he has made us, if he has redeemed us, if he has preserved us in being, it is but his due that we should be his servants.

And let me notice, next, that *this is the most honourable service that ever can be.* Did you say, "Lord, I am thy servant"? I see, coming like a flash of light from heaven, a bright spirit, and my imagination realizes his presence. There he stands, a living flame. It is a seraph fresh from the throne, and what does he say? "O Lord, I am thy servant." Are you not glad to enter into such company as this? When cherubim and seraphim count it their glory to be the servants of God, what man among us will think it to be a mean office? A prince, an emperor, if he be a sinner against God, is but a scullion in the kitchen compared with the true nobleman who serves the Lord in poverty and toil. This is the highest style of service under heaven: no courtier's honour can rival it. Knights of the Garter or what else you like lose their glories in comparison with the man whom God will call servant in the day of the appearing of our Lord and Saviour Jesus Christ. You are in grand company, young friend, if you are a servant of God.

And let me note, again, that *this service is full of beneficence.* If I had to engage in a trade, I should like to spend my time and strength in a pursuit which did no hurt to anybody, and did good to many. Somehow, I do not think that I should like to deal in deadly weapons—certainly not in the accursed drink. I would sooner starve than earn my bread by selling that or anything else that would debase my fellow-men, and degrade them below the level of brute beasts. It is a grand thing, I think, if a young man can follow a calling in which he may do well for himself, and be doing well to others at the same time. It is a fine thing to act as some have done who have not grown rich by grinding the faces of poor needlewomen, or by stinting the wage of the servant behind the counter, but have lifted others up with them, and as they have advanced, those in their employment have advanced also. That is a something worth living for in the lower sphere of things. But he that becomes a servant of God is doing good all along, for there is no part of the service of God which can do any harm to anybody. The service of the Lord is all goodness. It is good for yourself, and it is good for your fellow-men; for what does God ask in his service but that we should love him with all our heart, and that we love our neighbour as ourselves? He who does this is truly serving God by the help of his Spirit, and he is also greatly blessing men. I say, it is a most beneficent work to engage in; and therefore it is that I commend it to you—for its reasonableness, its honourableness, and its beneficence.

And there is another thought. *It is the most remunerative work under heaven.* "Not always to-day," someone may say. Yet I venture to say, "Always to-day." To serve God is remunerative *now*. How so? Certainly not in hard cash, as misers rightly call their gold; but in better material. A quiet conscience is better than gold; and to know that you are doing good is something more sweet in life than to know that you are getting rich or famous. Have not some of us lived long enough to know that the greater part of the things of this world are so much froth upon the top of the cup, far better blown away than preserved? The chief joy of life is to be right with yourself, your neighbour, your God. And he that gets right with God—what more does he want? He is paid for anything that he may suffer in the cause of God by his own peace of mind. There was a martyr once in Switzerland standing barefooted on the fagots, and about to be burnt quick to the death—no pleasant prospect for him. He accosted the magistrate who was superintending his execution, and asked him to come near him. He said, "Will you please to lay your hand upon my heart. I am about to die by fire. Lay your hand on my heart. If it beats any faster than it ordinarily beats, do not believe my religion." The magistrate, with palpitating heart himself, and all in a tremble, laid his hand upon the martyr's bosom, and found that he was just as calm as if he was going to his bed rather than to the flames. That is a grand thing! To wear in your button-hole that little flower called "heart's-ease," and to have the jewel of contentment in your bosom—this is heaven begun below : godliness is great gain to him that hath it.

But, listen. I think that all that we can get in this world is paltry, because we must leave it, or it must leave us in a very short time. I am addressing now a congregation of young men. Young men—but in how very short a time, if you all live, will your hair be powdered with the grey of age! In how brief an interval will the whole company now gathered in Exeter Hall be gathered in the grave! How short life is! How swift is time! The older we get the faster years fly. That only is worth my having which I can have for ever. That only is worth my grasping which death cannot tear out of my hand. The supreme reward of being a servant of God is hereafter; and if, young man, you should serve God and you should meet with losses here for Christ's sake, you may count these "light afflictions which are but for a moment," and think them quite unworthy to be compared with the glory that shall be revealed ; for there is a resurrection of the dead; there is a judgment to come; there is a life eternal; there is a heaven of unutterable splendour ; there is a place in that heaven for everyone of us who become true servants of the living God.

I think that I hear somebody saying, "Well, I do not want to be a servant." You cannot help it, my friend: you cannot help it. *You must be a servant of somebody.* "Then I will serve myself," says one. Pardon me, brave sir, if I whisper in your ear that if you serve yourself you will serve a fool. The man who is the servant of himself—listen to this sentence—the man who is the servant of himself is the slave of a slave; and I cannot imagine a more degrading position for a man to be in than to be the slave of a slave. You will assuredly serve some-body. You will wear fetters, too, if you serve the master that most men choose. Oh, but look at this city—this city full of free men; do the most of them know real liberty? Look at this city full of "free-thinkers." Is there any man that thinks in chains like the man who calls himself a free-thinker? Is there any man so credulous as the man that will not believe the Bible? He swallows a ton of difficulties, and yet complains that we have swallowed an ounce of them. He has much more need of faith of a certain sort than we have, for scepticism has far harder problems than faith. And look at the free-liver, what a bondage is his life? "Who hath woe? who hath redness of eyes" but the slave of strong drink? Who has rottenness in the bones but the slave of his passions? Is there any wretch that ever tugged in the Spanish galley, or any bondsman beneath the sun, that is half such a slave as he who will be led to-night of his lusts like a bullock to the slaughter, going to his own damnation, and even to the ruin of his body, while he makes himself the victim of his own passions? If I must be a slave, I will be a slave to Turk or savage, but never to myself, for that were the nethermost abyss of degradation. You must be a servant to some-body; there is no getting through the world without it, and if you are the servant to yourself, your bondage will be terrible. "Choose you this day whom ye will serve," for serve ye must. Every man must get him to his task, whether he be peer or pauper, millionaire or beggar. Kings and queens are usually the most wearied servants of all. The higher men climb, the more they have to serve their fellow-men. You must serve. Oh, that you would enter the service of your God!

There is room in it. Other places are crowded. Hundreds of young men go from shop to shop, and beg for the opportunity to earn a liveli-hood; I lament that in many instances they beg in vain. Some of you wear the boots from off your feet in trying to get something to do: how anxiously do I desire that you may find the employment you seek! But there is room in the service of God, and he is willing to receive you. And let me tell you that, if you enter his service, *it will help you in everything that you have to do in this life.* They say that a Christian man is a fool. Ah! proud opposers, though we say not the same to you, we might, perhaps, with truth think so. I have seen many believers in Jesus whom it would have been very dangerous to deal with as with fools, for very soon he that dealt with them in that fashion would have found that he made a great mistake. They are not always fools who are called so; they are such sometimes who use those names. I like a Christian man to be all the better in every respect for being a Christian. He should be a better servant and a better master. He should be a better tradesman and a better artisan. Surely, there is no poet whose min-strelsy excels that of the poet of the sanctuary: Milton still sits alone. There is no painter that should paint so well as he who tries with his brush to make immortal the memorable scenes in which great deeds were done. That which you can now do well you might do better by becoming a servant of God.

Thus would I commend my Master's service with all my heart. Are there any here who will enlist in it? for, if so, I have a second point to dwell on very briefly. I lift the flag and bid you rally to it, but first hear me patiently.

II. My second point is A WORD OF CAUTION. Did you notice that

David said, " O Lord, *truly* I am thy servant." "Truly." The word of
caution is, If you become the servant of God, become the servant of
God *truly*. God is not mocked. It is the curse of our churches that we
have so many merely nominal Christians in them. It is the plague of
this age that so many put on Christ's livery, and yet never do him a
hand's turn. Oh, if you serve God, mean it! If a man serves the devil,
let him serve the devil; but if he serves God, let him serve God. Some
people serve their business very actively, but not their God. There was,
years ago, a brother who used to pray at the prayer-meeting occasionally
in a low tone, as if he had no lungs left. Seldom could you hear
what he said, and if you listened and strained your ear there was still
nothing to hear. I thought that the brother had a bad voice, and so
I never called on him to pray any more. But, stepping one day into his
shop, I heard him say in a commanding voice, " John, fetch that half-
hundred!" "Oh, dear!" I thought, " that is the kind of voice he has in
his business, but when he comes into the service of God, that little squeak
is all he can give." Laugh again, sirs! Laugh again! It deserves to
be laughed at. But is there not much of this hypocrisy abroad? God
is to have the cheese-parings of a man's life, and he flings these
down as if they were all that God was worth. But as for the world,
that is to have the vigour of his life and the cream of his being. God
does not want nominal servants; nor do I invite them in his name
to-night. " O Lord, truly I am thy servant," said David ; and he that
does not mean to be *truly* God's servant, let him not pretend to be one
at all.

If you would be God's servant, then *count the cost.* You must leave
all others. "Ye cannot serve God and mammon." Ye cannot serve
Christ and Belial. He is not God's who is not God's only.

You must enter upon God's service also *for life ;* not to be sometimes
God's servant and sometimes not—off and on. Have you never heard
of the child who was asked by the district visitor, " Is your father a
Christian ?" The child replied, " Yes, sir, father is a Christian, but he
is not doing much at it just now." Oh, how many Christians there are
of that sort ! They profess to be Christians, but they are not doing
much at it. If you become the servant of God you must be his servant
every day and all the day for ever and ever.

> "'Tis done, the great transaction's done :
> I am my Lord's, and he is mine,"

must be a covenant declaration which must stand true throughout the
entire life. And if you become the servant of God *you must cease from
every known sin.* You cannot give one hand to Christ and another to
Satan. You must give up the dearest sins. Sweet sin must become bitter.
If sins are like right hands or right eyes they must be cut off or plucked
out, and you must follow Christ fully, giving him all your heart, and
soul, and strength ; for if it be not so, you cannot be his disciple.

So much by way of caution. I am very brief on that, but take it as
though it were said at length.

III. I want now to OFFER COUNSEL IN THE MATTER OF DISTINCT
CONFESSION IF YOU BECOME THE SERVANT OF CHRIST. "I am thy

servant," says David ; and then he puts it over again, "I *am* thy servant."

Now, I want every young man here who is a Christian to make it known by an open avowal of his discipleship. I mean that there should not be one among us who follows the Lord Jesus Christ in a mean, sneaking, indistinct, questionable way. It has become the custom of many to try to be Christians and never say anything about it. This is beneath contempt. But I urge you true servants of Christ to " out with it," and never to be ashamed, because if ever a bold profession was required it is required now. You may not be burned at the stake for saying that you are a Christian, but I believe that the old enmity to Christ is not removed, and a true believer will still be called upon to take up the cross. In many a house in London a young man will have to run the gauntlet if he is known to be a Christian. Run the gauntlet, then ! You have an honourable opportunity. It is a grand thing to be permitted to endure reproach for Christ's sake ; and you should look at it as a choice privilege that you are counted worthy not only to believe in the Lord Jesus Christ, but also to suffer for his sake. Nowadays the world wants decided men. Everywhere it seems to be imagined that you may believe what you like, or believe nothing ; and do as you like, or do nothing, and the result will be all the same both to the unbeliever and the man of faith. But it is not so. It is time for the out-and-out servant of the Lord to put down his foot and say, " I have believed ; therefore have I spoken. I am a Christian, and while I leave you to your individual liberty I mean to have mine, and I mean to exercise that liberty by being openly and unquestionably on the side of Christ, and on the side of that which is pure, and sober, and right, and true, and good."

Is not this well deserved by Christ? Oh, if he never was ashamed of us we never ought to be ashamed of him ! If the Lord of life and glory stooped to die for us, could we ever stoop at all even if we rolled into the mire or dropped into the grave for him ? Surely, our blessed Lord deserves to be followed by heroes. Every man in the presence of the cross-bearing Jesus should feel that to take up his cross and follow Christ is the simplest and most natural thing that can be; and he should resolve in God's strength that he will do it, and continue to obey the Lord, though all the world should ridicule. Let me tell you that *it is the easiest thing* to do, after all : as compared with compromise it is simplicity itself. I have known many young Christians that have come up to London, and they have determined that they would serve God if they could, but that they would keep it very quiet, and so they have attempted to be Christians on the sly : but they have failed. If you are a genuine Christian it will be found out as surely as you are a living man. If you go down to Mitcham when the lavender is ripe, you may shut all your windows, but you will find that the perfume of the lavender will get into your house somehow. Christianity has a perfume about it which will spread abroad, so that all in the house enquire, " What is all this?" The wicked wags will whisper that you are " a Christian young man"; and if you have not come out at first it will be very hard for you afterwards. Begin as you mean to go on, young man. Do not hide your flag and try to sail under false colours, for both good and bad will be against you in that case. You will be hunted from place to place if the dogs find that you will run: you will make rare sport for the hunters if you take to your heels. Come straight out and let them do their best or their worst. Live a most consistent life, and the other young fellows will know whereabouts you are. They will soon reckon you up, and if you are sincere before long they will let you alone: and if they do not, forbearance is still yours. If they continue to persecute you, so much the worse *for them;* for you, by your quiet, holy life, will make them feel that it is hard for them to kick against the pricks. But, anyhow, do come out bravely. Some of you young fellows are like rats behind the wainscot: you do not mind coming out of a night to eat the crumbs on the floor, but there you are, back again directly: I mean that you will join in religious exercises if it is not known to the shop, but you would not for the world become suspected of real religion. Is that how true Christians should act? No; put on your livery. "But I do not care about joining a church," says one. Very likely; but do you not know that it is found to be a convenient and proper thing in warfare that a soldier should wear regimentals? At first Oliver Cromwell's Ironsides were dressed any-how and everyhow; but in the *mêlée* with the Cavaliers it sometimes happened that an Ironside was struck down by mistake by the sword of one of his own brethren, and so the general said, "You wear red coats, all of you. We must know our own men from the enemy." What Cromwell said he meant, and they had to come in their red coats, for it is found essential in warfare that men should be known by some kind of regimental. Now, you that are Christ's, do not go about as if you were ashamed of his Majesty's service. Put on your red coats: I mean come out as acknowledged Christians. Unite with a body of Christian people, and be distinctly known to be Christ's. How are the ordinances of the Lord's house to be sustained if every man is to go to heaven alone by the back way? Come out boldly. If any man wants to laugh at a Christian, step out, and say, "Laugh at me. If anybody wants to abuse a fellow, and call him a hypocrite, a Presbyterian, a Methodist, come on! I am ready for you." If you have once done that, and come right out on the straight, you shall find it the easiest thing in life to bear the reproach of Christ.

And oh, remember, young men, that if you should meet with any reproach for Christ, *a reward awaits you.* Shall I tell you a parable? There was once a king's son who went upon a journey incognito, and he journeyed into a far country, but there he was ill-treated, and because of his language and his appearance the people of the land set him in the pillory, which was of old the place of scorn. They set him there, and the mob gathered round him, and threw all kinds of filth and ordure upon him. This prince unknown must needs be pelted thus, and made as the offscouring of all things. But there was among them one man who loved the prince, and who recognized him, and determined to bear him company. He mounted the pillory and stood by his side, and wiped his face with his handkerchief, and whenever he could he put himself in the way of the mire and dirt that he might catch it and screen the prince from it. Years went on, and it came to pass that the prince was back in his kingdom in all his glory, and the courtiers were standing round about the throne. This man who had been a poor man in his own country was summoned to the court, and when he arrived at the palace, the prince saw him, and said to the peers of the realm, "Stand aside and make way for this man. He was with me when I was ill-treated and scorned, and now he shall be with me in my glory, chief among you here." Do you not know the story of how our sweet Lord Jesus came down to earth and suffered many things, and how he was despised and rejected of men? Young man, are you the man who would wipe his blessed face and share his shame, and take half turns with the man of Nazareth in all the obloquy and scorn? Are you that man? Then there shall come a day when the great Father on his throne shall spy you out and say, "Make a lane, ye angels! Stand back, seraphim and cherubim! Make way for this man. He was with my Son in his humiliation, and now he shall be with him in his glory." Will you receive that mark of honour? Not unless you are prepared to put on the badge of Christ, and say, "I am his servant and his follower from this day to life's end." God help you to do it! O Holy Spirit, lead scores of young men now to shoulder the cross!

IV. And so, lest I weary you, I CLOSE BY CONGRATULATING SOME OF YOU who are God's servants UPON YOUR FREEDOM, for that is the last part of the text. "Truly I am thy servant; I am thy servant, and the son of thine handmaid: *thou hast loosed my bonds.*"

Oh, but this is a grand thing—this loosing of the bonds. Were you ever in bonds? Did you ever feel *the bonds of guilt?* Are you believing in Christ: then those bonds are loosed, for your sin is forgiven you for Christ's sake, and you are delivered from all condemnation. Oh, will you not love him who has loosed your bonds? Were you, dear friend, ever in *the bonds of despondency* and despair on account of sin? Did you ever sit and sigh because you thought that there was no salvation for you? And did the Lord Jesus Christ appear to you as your crucified Saviour? And did you trust in him, and feel the bonds of despondency broken? Happy day for you! I remember it well myself. Oh, then, will you not follow him that has loosed your bonds? Now, you are clean delivered from the bonds of guilt and despair, you are also saved from *the power of sin.* The habits that were your masters are now destroyed. The lusts that lorded it over you are now slain; and you are free. Will you not wish to be bound to Christ henceforth because he has loosed your bonds? I know some men in this world who talk a great deal about being free, but they are always in chains. There is a man I know for whom the devil makes a nauseous mixture; at least, to me it is very nauseous; and he says, "Drink a quart of it;" and he drinks. "Drink another," says the devil; and he does so. "Drink another," says the devil; and his brain begins to reel, and he is all on fire. "Drink it," says the devil; and he lets it run down his throat, for he is in chains. I know another who, against his better self, will go into sin, which he knows to be sin, and knows to be injurious to him. Yet he goes in a silly manner and harms himself more and more. He is led by the nose by the devil, and he says that he cannot resist. He is a slave in the worst sense. Oh, blessed is the man who can say, "Thou hast loosed my bonds: no evil habit enslaves me now, no passion controls me, no lust enchains me!" Young friend, if you can stand up and say, "I am free from myself: I am no longer the slave of sin!"—you are a blessed man, and you may well be God's servant for ever!

What a mercy it is to be delivered from *the bonds of the fear of man!* Some young men dare not call their souls their own for fear of their employers. A great many more are dreadfully in fear of the young man who sleeps in the next bed. Oh, dear, they dare not do what is right! Poor babies that they are, they must ask permission to keep a conscience! When they are about to do anything they are always saying, "What will So-and-so think of it?" Does it matter to any true man what all the world thinks about him? Has he not risen out of that? Is he still a serf? "Go," says the brave man; "think what you will, and say what you will. If I serve God, I am no servant of yours; by your censures I shall not fall, as by your praises I shall not rise." Be afraid of such a thing as I myself, and ask the leave of another man what I shall think, what I shall believe, what I shall do! I will die first! When God brings a man to know himself, and to be his servant, he sets him free from this cowardly crime of being afraid of a man that shall die.

So, too, he sets him free from all *the maxims and customs of the world.* Young man, when you go into business, they will tell you that you must do so-and-so, because it is "the custom of the trade." "Why," say you, "it is lying!" You will be told that it is not exactly lying, because your customer is used to your tricks, and quite understands that a hundred means eighty, and the best quality means a second-class article. I am told that half the business in London is robbery in some form or another if the customs of the trade are not understood. If it be so that it is all understood, it might just as well be done honestly for the matter of that, and it would pay as well. Yet, somehow, men feel as if they must do what others have done, or else they will be out of the race. Slaves! Serfs! Be honest! He is not free that dares not be honest. Shall I not speak my mind? Shall I not act out my integrity? If I cannot, then I cannot say with David, "Thou hast loosed my bonds."

Lastly, what a blessing it is when God frees us from *the fear of death!* "Thou hast loosed my bonds." What will it matter to you, young man, if you become the servant of God by faith in Jesus Christ whether you live or die? If you die early, so much the sooner in heaven. If you live long, so much the longer in which to serve your God on earth. Give your heart to Christ; trust your salvation in those dear hands that were pierced for sinners; thus become the servant of God, and you shall be provided for, for his children shall not lack. You shall be led, guided, taught, educated, prepared for heaven; and one of these bright days a convoy of celestial spirits shall think it an honour to be permitted to bear your joyful spirit up to the throne of God.

Who will be the servant of the Most High, then? I always wish when I have done with sermons that I could preach them over again, because I have not done well enough; but all I care to preach for is that I may touch your hearts. I would not care a snap of the fingers to be an orator, or to put sentences prettily. I want to put the truth so that some young man will say, "I will serve God." I remember young men that began life when I began, that are now—I will not say what. Ah! I remember hearing their names mentioned as models, they were such fine young men, and had just gone up to London. Yes, and they are to-night, if not in jail, in the workhouse. It all came about in this way: the young man sent word home to his mother what the text was on the Sunday, yet he had not been to hear a sermon at all. He had been to some amusement, to spend a happy day: wherever he went he had neglected the house of God; and by-and-by there was a little wrong in his small accounts—just a little matter; but that man could not pick himself up again, once having lost his character. There was another. There was nothing wrong in his accounts, but his habits were loose. By-and-by he was ill. Who could wonder? When a man plays with edged tools he is very likely to cut himself. It was not long before he was so sickly that he could not attend to business, and ere long he died; and they said—I fear it was true—that he killed himself by vice. And that is how thousands do in London. Oh, if you become the servant of God this will not happen to you! You may not be rich; you may not be famous; you may not be great: you need not want these things. They are gilded vanities full often. But to be a man—to the fulness of your manhood; to be free and dare to look every other man in the world in the face, and speak the truth, and do the right; to be a man that can look God in the face because Christ has covered him with his glorious righteousness—this is the ambition with which I would fire the spirit of every young man before me; and I pray God that the flame may burn in his life by the power of the divine Spirit. Come then, brethren, bow your heads and say, " We will be servants of the living God henceforth and for ever." God grant it, for Jesus Christ's sake. Amen and Amen.

9 The Blood of Sprinkling and the Children

"Then Moses called for all the elders of Israel, and said unto them, **Draw out and take** you a lamb according to your families, and kill the passover. And ye shall **take** a bunch of hyssop, and dip it in the blood that is in the bason, and strike the lintel and the two side posts with the blood that is in the bason; and none of you shall go out at the door of his house until the morning. For the Lord will pass through to smite the Egyptians: and when he seeth the blood upon the lintel, and on the two side posts, the Lord will pass over the door, and will not suffer the destroyer to come in unto your houses to smite you. And ye shall observe this thing for an ordinance to thee and to thy sons for ever. And it shall come to pass, when ye be come to the land which the Lord will give you, according as he hath promised, that ye shall keep this service. And it shall come to pass, when your children shall say unto you, What mean ye by this service? that ye shall say, It is the sacrifice of the Lord's passover, who passed over the houses of the children of Israel in Egypt, when he smote the Egyptians, and delivered our houses."—Exodus xii. 21—27.

I WANTED, dear friends, earnestly wanted, to continue the subject of last Lord's-day morning; for I felt it important that we should bear again and again our witness to the doctrine of the vicarious sacrifice of Jesus Christ our Lord. But, at the same time, I promised that I would endeavour to keep "the feast of the children," and have a sermon which should be specially addressed to Sunday-school teachers. I could not preach a school sermon at the appointed time, so as to open your children's week, but thought a discourse might come in none the less suitably if I brought up the rear by closing your meetings. How am I to fulfil both my purposes? I think the subject before us will enable me to do so. We shall preach of the sprinkled blood, and of Jesus the great sacrifice for sin; and then we shall press upon all who know the value of the great redemption that they teach the young in their earliest days what is meant by the death of Jesus and salvation through his blood.

The Paschal lamb was a special type of our Lord Jesus Christ. We are not left to gather this from the general fact that all the ancient sacrifices were shadows of the one true and real substance; but we are assured in the New Testament that "Christ our passover is sacrificed for us" (1 Cor. v. 7). As the Paschal lamb must be without blemish, so was our Lord, and its killing and roasting with fire were typical of his death and sufferings. Even as to time, our Lord fulfilled the type, for the time of his crucifixion was the passover. As the impression answers to the seal, so does the sacrifice of our Lord correspond with all the items

99

of the passover ceremonial. We see him "drawn out" from among men, and led as a lamb to the slaughter; we see his blood shed and sprinkled; we see him roasted in the fire of anguish; by faith we eat of him, and flavour the feast with the bitter herbs of penitence. We see Jesus and salvation where the carnal eye sees only a slaughtered lamb, and a people saved from death.

The Spirit of God in the passover ceremonial lays special emphasis upon *the sprinkling of the blood*. That which men so greatly oppose, he as diligently sets forth as the head and front of revelation. The blood of the chosen lamb was caught in a basin, and not spilled upon the ground in wastefulness; for the blood of Christ is most precious. Into this bowl of blood a bunch of hyssop was dipped. The sprays of that little shrub would hold the crimson drops, so that they could be easily sprinkled. Then the father of the family went outside, and struck with this hyssop the lintel and the two side posts of the door; and so the house was marked with three crimson streaks. No blood was put upon the threshold. Woe unto the man that tramples upon the blood of Christ, and treats it as an unholy thing! Alas! I fear that many are doing so at this hour, not only among the outside world, but among those who profess and call themselves Christians.

I shall endeavour to bring forward two things. First, *the importance attached to the sprinkled blood*; and, secondly, *the institution connected with it*, namely, that the children should be instructed in the meaning of sacrifice, so that they also may teach their children, and keep alive the memory of the Lord's great deliverance.

I. First: THE IMPORTANCE ATTACHED TO THE BLOOD OF SACRIFICE is here made very plain. Pains are taken to make the sacrifice observable, yea, to force it upon the notice of all the people.

I note, first, that *it became and remained the national mark.* If you had traversed the streets of Memphis or Rameses on the night of the Passover, you could have told who were Israelites and who were Egyptians by one conspicuous token. There was no need to listen under the window to hear the speech of the people within the house, nor to wait till any came into the street so that you could observe their attire. This one thing alone would be a sufficient guide—the Israelite had the blood-mark upon his doorway, the Egyptian had it not. Mark you, this is still the great point of difference between the children of God and the children of the wicked one. There are, in truth, but two denominations upon this earth—the church and the world; those who are justified in Christ Jesus, and those who are condemned in their sins. This shall stand for a never-failing sign of the "Israelite indeed": he has come to the blood of sprinkling, which speaketh better things than that of Abel. He that believeth in the Son of God, as the one accepted sacrifice for sin, hath salvation, and he that believeth not in him will die in his sins. The true Israel are trusting in the sacrifice once offered for sin; it is their rest, their comfort, their hope. As for those who are not trusting in the atoning sacrifice, they have rejected the counsel of God against themselves, and thus have declared their true character and condition. Jesus said, "Ye believe not, because ye are not of my sheep, as I said unto you"; and want of faith in that shedding of blood, without which there is no remission of sin, is the damning mark

of one who is a stranger to the commonwealth of Israel. Let us make
no question about it: "Whosoever goeth onward and abideth not in
the teaching of Christ, hath not God." (See 2 John 9, in the Revised
Version.) He that will not accept the propitiation which God hath
set forth must bear his own iniquity. Nothing more just, and yet
nothing more terrible, can happen to such a man than that his
iniquity should not be purged by sacrifice nor offering for ever. I
care not what your supposed righteousness may be, nor how you think
to commend yourselves to God, if you reject his Son, he will reject *you*.
If you come before God without the atoning blood, you have neither
part nor lot in the matter of the covenant inheritance, and you are not
numbered among the people of God. The sacrifice is the national mark
of the spiritual Israel, and he that hath it not is an alien; he shall have
no inheritance among them that are sanctified, neither shall he behold
the Lord in glory.

Secondly, as this was the national mark, *it was also the saving token.*
That night the Angel of Death spread his wings on the blast, and as
he flew down the streets of Egypt he smote high and low, the firstborn of princes and the first-born of beasts, so that in every house
and in every stall there was one dead. Where he saw the blood-mark he
entered not to smite; but everywhere else the vengeance of the Lord fell
on the rebellious. The words are very remarkable: "The Lord will
pass over the door, and will not suffer the destroyer to come in unto
your houses to smite you." What holds back the sword? Nothing but
the blood-stain on the door. The lamb has been slain, and they have
sprinkled their houses with the blood, and therefore are they secure.
The sons of Jacob were not richer, nor wiser, nor stronger, nor more
skilled than the sons of Ham; but they were redeemed by the blood,
and therefore they lived, while those who knew not the redeeming token
died. When Jericho fell down, the one house that stood was that which
had the scarlet line in the window; and when the Lord visits for sin,
the man that shall escape is he who knows Jesus, "in whom we have
redemption through his blood, the forgiveness of sin according to the
riches of his grace."

I call your very special attention, however, to the words that are
used in the twenty-third verse: "The Lord will pass through to smite
the Egyptians; and when he seeth the blood upon the lintel, and on the
two side posts, the Lord will pass over the door." What an instructive
expression! "When *he* seeth the blood." It is a very comforting thing
for you and for me to behold the atonement; for thus we gain peace
and enter into rest; but, after all, the grand reason of our salvation is
that the Lord himself looks upon the atonement, and is well pleased for
his righteousness' sake. In the thirteenth verse we hear the Lord
himself say: "When I see the blood I will pass over you." Think of
the holy eye of God being turned to him that taketh away the sin of
the world, and so fixed on him that he passes over us. He is of purer
eyes than to behold iniquity, but he looks upon the face of his anointed
and forgives the sin. He accepts us with our sacrifice. Well does our
hymn-writer pray—

> "Him and then the sinner see;
> Look through Jesu's wounds on me."

It is not *our* sight of the sprinkled blood which is the basis of salvation, but *God's* sight of it. God's acceptance of Christ is the sure guarantee of the salvation of those who accept his sacrifice. Beloved, when thine eye of faith is dim, when thine eye-balls swim in a flood of tears, when the darkness of sorrow hides much from thy vision, then Jehovah sees the blood of his Son and spares thee. In the thick darkness, when thou canst not see at all, the Lord God never fails to see in Jesus that with which he is well pleased, and with which his law is honoured. He will not suffer the destroyer to come near thee to harm thee, because he sees in Christ that which vindicates his justice and establishes the needful rule of law. The blood is the saving mark. At this moment this is the pressing question for each one in the company gathered in this house: Do you trust the divine propitiation or do you not? Bring to me what you will to prove your own personal excellence. I believe in no virtue which insults the Saviour's blood, which alone cleanseth us from all sin. Rather confess your multiplied transgressions and shortcomings, and then take heart and hope; for there is forgiveness large and free for the very chief of sinners, through him who has made peace by the blood of his cross.

O my hearer, guilty and self-condemned, if thou wilt now come and trust in Jesus Christ, thy sins, which are many, shall be all forgiven thee, and thou shalt love so much in return, that the whole bent and bias of thy mind shall be turned from sin to gracious obedience. The atonement applied to the conscience saves from despair, and then acting upon the heart it saves from the love of evil. But the atonement is the saving sign. The blood on the lintel and on the two side posts secured the house of the poorest Israelite; but the proudest Egyptian, yea, even Pharaoh on the throne, could not escape the destroyer's sword. Believe and live. Reject the atonement and perish!

Note, next, that *the mark of the blood was rendered as conspicuous as possible.* The Israelites, though they ate the Paschal lamb in the quiet of their own families, yet made no secret of the sacrifice. They did not make the distinctive mark upon the wall of some inner chamber, or in some place where they could cover it with hangings, that no man might perceive it; but they smote the upper part of the doorway and the two side posts of the door, so that all who passed by the house must see that it was marked in a peculiar manner, and marked with blood. The Lord's people were not ashamed to have the blood thus put in the forefront of every dwelling: and those that are saved by the great sacrifice are not to treat the doctrine of substitution as a hole-and-corner creed, to be secretly held, but not openly avowed. The death of Jesus in our room and place and stead is not a redemption of which we are ashamed to speak in any place. Call it old-fashioned and out of date, our critics may; but we are not ashamed to publish it to the four winds of heaven, and to avow our confidence in it. He that is ashamed of Christ in this generation, of him will Christ be ashamed when he comes in the glory of his Father, and all his holy angels with him. There is a theology abroad in the world which admits the death of Christ to a certain indefinable place in its system, but that place is very much in the rear: I claim for the atonement the front and the centre. The Lamb must be in the midst of the throne.

Atonement is not a mystery scarcely to be spoken of, or if spoken of at all, to be whispered. No, no, it is a sublime simplicity, a fact for a child to know, a truth for the common people to rejoice in! We must preach Christ crucified whatever else we do not preach. Brethren, I do not think a man ought to hear a minister preach three sermons without learning the doctrine of atonement. I give wide latitude when I say this, for I would desire never to preach at all without setting forth salvation by faith in the blood of Jesus. Across my pulpit and my tabernacle shall be the mark of the blood ; it will disgust the enemy, but it will delight the faithful. Substitution seems to me to be the soul of the gospel, the life of the gospel, the essence of the gospel ; therefore must it be ever in the front. Jesus, as the Lamb of God, is the Alpha, and we must keep him first and before all others. I charge you, Christian people, do not make this a secondary doctrine. Keep your perspective right, and have this always in the foreground. Other truths are valuable, and may most worthily be placed in the distance ; but this is always to be in the foreground. The centre of Christianity is the cross, and the meaning of the cross is substitution.

> "We may not know, we cannot tell,
> What pains our Jesus bare,
> But we believe it was for us
> He hung and suffered there."

The great sacrifice is the place of gathering for the chosen seed : we meet at the cross, even as every family in Israel met around the table whereon was placed the lamb, and met within a house which was marked with blood. Instead of looking upon the vicarious sacrifice as placed somewhere in the remote distance, we find in it the centre of the church. Nay, more ; it is so much the vital, all-essential centre, that to remove it is to tear out the heart of the church. A congregation which has rejected the sacrifice of Christ is not a church, but an assembly of unbelievers. Of the church I may truly say, "The blood is the life thereof." Like the doctrine of justification by faith, the doctrine of a vicarious sacrifice is the article of standing or falling to each church : atonement by the substitutionary sacrifice of Christ means spiritual life, and the rejection of it is the reverse. Wherefore, we must never be ashamed of this all-important truth, but make it as conspicuous as possible. "For the preaching of the cross is to them that perish foolishness ; but unto us which are saved it is the power of God."

Further, the sprinkled blood was not only most conspicuous, but *it was made very dear to the people themselves by the fact that they trusted in it in the most implicit manner.* After the door-posts had been smeared the people went inside into their houses, and they shut to the door, never to open it again till the morning. They were busy inside : there was the roasting of the lamb, the preparing of the bitter herbs, the girding of their loins, the getting ready for their march, and so forth ; but this was done without fear of danger, though they knew that the destroyer was abroad. The command of the Lord was, "None of you shall go out at the door of his house until the morning." What is going on in the street ? You must not go to see. The midnight hour has

come. Did you not hear it ? Hark, that dreadful cry ! Again a
piercing shriek ! What is it ? The anxious mother asks, "What can
it be ?" "There was a great cry in Egypt." The Israelites must not
heed that cry so as to break the divine word which shut them in for
a little moment, till the tempest was overpast. Perhaps persons of
doubtful mind, during that dread night, may have said, "Something
awful is happening. Hear those cries ! Listen to the tramping of the
people in the streets, as they hurry to and fro ! It may be there is
a conspiracy to slay us at dead of night." "None of you shall go out
at the door of his house until the morning" was sufficient for all
who truly believed. They were safe, and they knew it, and so,
like the chicks beneath the wings of the hen, they rested in safety.
Beloved, let us do the same. Let us honour the precious blood of
Christ not only by speaking of it boldly to others, but by a calm
and happy trust in it for ourselves. In full assurance let us rest.
Do you believe that Jesus died for you ? Then be at peace. Let
no man's heart fail him now that he knows that Jesus died for our
sins according to the Scriptures. Let the cross be the pillar of our
confidence, unmoved and immovable. Do not be agitated about
what has been or what is to be: we are housed in safety in Christ
Jesus both from the sins of the past and the dangers of the future. All
is well, since love's atoning work is done. In holy peacefulness let us
proceed with our household work, purging out the old leaven and keeping the feast ; but let no fear or doubt disturb us for an instant. We
pity those who die without Christ, but we cannot quit our Lord
under the pretence of saving them : that would be folly. I know there
are terrible cries outside in the streets—who has not heard them ? Oh,
that the people would but shelter beneath the blood-mark ! It pierces
our heart to think of the doom of the ungodly when they perish in their
sins ; but, as Noah did not quit the ark, nor Israel leave her abode, so
our hope is not larger than the cross will warrant. All who shelter
beneath the blood of the atonement are secure, and as for those who
reject this great salvation, how shall they escape ? There are great and
sad mysteries in this long night, but in the morning we shall know as
much of God's dealings with men as it will be good for us to know.
Meanwhile, let us labour to bring our fellows within the pale of safety,
but yet let us be ourselves peaceful, composed, restful, and joyful.
"There is therefore now no condemnation to them which are in Christ
Jesus." "Therefore being justified by faith, we have peace with God
through our Lord Jesus Christ." "And not only so, but we also joy
in God through our Lord Jesus Christ, by whom we have now received
the atonement." Possess ye your souls in patience. Oh, rest in the Lord,
and wait patiently for him. Feed upon the Lamb, for his flesh is meat
indeed. That same Jesus who has preserved your life from destruction
will be the sustenance of that life evermore. Be happy beneath the
saving blood-mark. Make a feast of your passover. Though there be
death outside, let your joy be undisturbed.

I cannot stay long on any one point, and therefore notice, next, that
the Paschal bloodshedding was to be had in perpetual remembrance. "Ye
shall observe this thing for an ordinance to thee and to thy sons for
ever." As long as Israel remained a people, they were to keep the

passover: so long as there is a Christian upon earth the sacrificial death of the Lord Jesus must be kept in memory. No progress of years or advance of thought could take away the memory of the Paschal sacrifice from Israel. Truly it was a night to be remembered when the Lord brought out his people from under the iron yoke of Egypt. It was such a wonderful deliverance, as to the plagues which preceded it, and the miracle at the Red Sea which followed it, that no event could possibly excel it in interest and glory. It was such a triumph of God's power over the pride of Pharaoh, and such a manifestation of God's love to his own people, that they were not merely to be glad for one night, nor for one year, nor even for a century; but they were to remember it for ever. Might there not come a time when Israel would have achieved further history? Might not some grander event eclipse the glory of Egypt's overthrow? Never! The death of Egypt's firstborn, and the song of Moses at the Red Sea must remain for ever woven into the tapestry of Hebrew history. Evermore did Jehovah say, "I am the Lord thy God, which have brought thee out of the land of Egypt, out of the house of bondage." Beloved, the death of our Lord Jesus Christ is to be declared and showed by us until he come. No truth can ever be discovered which can put his sacrificial death into the shade. Whatever shall occur, even though he cometh in the clouds of heaven, yet our song shall be for ever, "Unto him that loved us and washed us from our sins in his own blood." Amid the splendour of his endless reign he shall be "the Lamb in the midst of the throne." Christ as the sacrifice for sin shall ever be the subject of our hallelujahs: "For thou wast slain." Certain vainglorious minds are advancing—advancing from the rock to the abyss. They are making progress from truth to falsehood. They are thinking, but their thoughts are not God's thoughts, neither are their ways his ways. They are leaving the gospel, they are going away from Christ, and they know not whither. In quitting the substitutionary sacrifice they are quitting the sole hope of man. As for us, we hear the Lord saying to us, "Ye shall observe this thing for an ordinance to thee and to thy sons for ever," and so will we do. "Jesus Christ, the same yesterday, to-day, and for ever," is our boast and glory. Let others wander where they will, we abide with him who bore our sins in his own body on the tree.

Notice next, dear friends, that when the people came into the land where no Egyptian ever entered they were still to remember the passover. "It shall come to pass, when ye be come to the land which the Lord will give you, according as he hath promised, that ye shall keep this service." In the land that flowed with milk and honey there was still to be the memorial of the sprinkled blood. Our Lord Jesus is not for the first day of our repentance only, but for all the days of our lives: we remember him as well amid our highest spiritual joys as in our deepest spiritual griefs. The Paschal lamb is for Canaan, as well as for Egypt, and the sacrifice for sin is for our full assurance as well as for our trembling hope. You and I will never attain to such a state of grace that we can do without the blood which cleanseth from sin. If we should ever reach perfection, then would Christ be even more precious than he is to-day; or, if we did not find him so, we might be sure that our pretended attainment was a wretched delusion. If we walk in the light as God is in the light, and have constant fellowship with him, yet still the blood of Jesus Christ his Son cleanseth us from all sin.

Moreover, brethren, I want you to notice carefully that *this sprinkling of the blood was to be an all-pervading memory.* Catch this thought : the children of Israel could not go out of their houses, and they could not come in, without the remembrance of the sprinkled blood. It was over their heads; they must come under it. It was on the right hand and on the left : they must be surrounded by it. They might almost say of it, " Whither shall we go from thy presence ? " Whether they looked on their own doors, or on those of their neighbours, there was the same threefold streak, and it was there both by day and by night. Nor was this all; when two of Israel married, and the foundation of a family was laid, there was another memorial. The young husband and wife had the joy of looking upon their firstborn child, and then they called to mind that the Lord had said, " Sanctify to me all the firstborn." As an Israelite he explained this to his son, and said, " By strength of hand the Lord brought us out from Egypt, from the house of bondage : and it came to pass, when Pharaoh would hardly let us go, that the Lord slew all the firstborn in the land of Egypt, both the firstborn of man, and the firstborn of beast: therefore I sacrifice to the Lord all that openeth the matrix, being males ; but all the firstborn of my children I redeem." The commencement of every family that made up the Israelitish nation was thus a time of special remembrance of the sprinkling of the blood; for then the redemption money must be paid, and thus an acknowledgment made that they were the Lord's, having been bought with a price. In ways many, and everywhere present, the people were reminded of the need of sacrifice. To the thoughtful, every going down of the sun reminded him of the night to be remembered ; while the beginning of each year in the month Abib brought home to him the fact that the beginning of his nation dated from the time of the killing of the lamb. The Lord took means to keep this matter before the people ; for they were wayward, and seemed bent upon forgetting, even like this present age.

In the thirteenth chapter, in verse 9, we read : " It shall be for a sign unto thee upon thine hand, and for a memorial between thine eyes." And again, in verse 16, we read : " And it shall be for a token upon thine hand, and for frontlets between thine eyes : for by strength of hand the Lord brought us forth out of Egypt." By this is meant that they were henceforth to do everything with regard to redemption, and they were henceforth to see everything in connection with redemption. Redemption by blood was to consecrate each man's hand, so that he could not use it for evil, but must employ it for the Lord. He could not take his food, or his tool, in his hand, without remembrance of the sprinkled blood which had made his food and his labour a blessing. All his acts were to be under the influence of atoning blood. Oh, what service you and I would render if it was always redeemed labour that we gave ! If we went to our Sunday-school class, for instance, feeling, " I am bought with a price," and if we preached with redeemed lips the gospel of our own salvation, how livingly and lovingly we should speak! What an effect this would have on our lives! You would not dare, some of you, to do what you now do, if you remembered that Jesus died for you. Many a thing which you have left undone would at once be minded if you had a clearer consciousness of redeeming love. The Jews became superstitious, and were content with the letter of their law, and so they wrote out certain verses upon little strips of parchment called " tephillin," which they enclosed in a box, and then strapped upon their wrists. The true meaning of the passage did not lie in any such childish action; but it taught them that they were to labour and to act with holy hands, as men under overwhelming obligations to the Lord's redeeming grace. Redemption is to be our impulse for holy service, our check when we are tempted to sin. They were also to wear the memory of the passover as frontlets between their eyes, and you know how certain Jews actually wore phylacteries upon their foreheads. That could be no more than the mere shell of the thing: the essence of the command was that they were to look on everything in reference to redemption by blood. Brethren, we should view everything in this world by the light of redemption, and then we shall view it aright. It makes a wonderful change whether you view providence from the standpoint of human merit or from the foot of the cross. We see nothing truly till Jesus is our light. Everything is seen in its reality when you look through the glass, the ruby glass of the atoning sacrifice. Use this telescope of the cross, and you shall see far and clear ; look at sinners through the cross ; look at saints through the cross; look at sin through the cross ; look at the world's joys and sorrows through the cross ; look at heaven and hell through the cross. See how conspicuous the blood of the passover was meant to be, and then learn from all this to make much of the sacrifice of Jesus, yea, to make everything of it, for Christ is all.

One thing more : we read in Deuteronomy, in the sixth chapter, and the eighth verse, concerning the commandments of the Lord, as follows: " And thou shalt bind them for a sign upon thine hand, and they shall be as frontlets between thine eyes. And thou shalt write them upon the posts of thy house, and on thy gates." See, then, that the law is to be written hard by the memorials of the blood. In Switzerland, in the Protestant villages, you have seen texts of Scripture upon the doorposts. I half wish we had that custom in England. How much of gospel might be preached to wayfarers if texts of Scripture were over Christian people's doors ! It might be ridiculed as Pharisaical, but we could get over that. Few are liable to that charge in these days through being religious overmuch. I like to see texts of Scripture in our houses, in all the rooms, on the cornices, and on the walls ; but outside on the door—what a capital advertisement the gospel might get at a cheap rate ! But note, that when the Jew wrote upon his door-posts a promise, or a precept, or a doctrine, he had to write upon a surface stained with blood, and when the next year's passover came round he had to sprinkle the blood with the hyssop right over the writing. It seems to me so delightful to think of the law of God in connection with that atoning sacrifice which has magnified it and made it honourable. God's commands come to me as a redeemed man; his promises are to me as a blood-bought man; his teaching instructs me as one for whom atonement has been made. The law in the hand of Christ is not a sword to slay us, but a jewel to enrich us. All truth taken in connection with the cross is greatly enhanced in value. Holy Scripture itself becomes dear to a sevenfold degree when we see that it comes to us as the redeemed of the Lord, and bears upon its every page marks of those dear hands which were nailed to the tree for us.

Beloved, you now see how everything was done that could well be thought of to bring the blood of the Paschal lamb into a high position in the esteem of the people whom the Lord brought out of Egypt; and you and I must do everything we can think of to bring forward, and keep before men for ever the precious doctrine of the atoning sacrifice of Christ. He was made sin for us though he knew no sin, that we might be made the righteousness of God in him.

II. And now I will spend a short time in reminding you of THE INSTITUTION THAT WAS CONNECTED WITH THE REMEMBRANCE OF THE PASSOVER. "It shall come to pass, when your children shall say unto you, What mean ye by this service? that ye shall say, It is the sacrifice of the Lord's passover."

Inquiry should be excited in the minds of our children. Oh, that we could get them to ask questions about the things of God! Some of them enquire very early, others of them seem diseased with much the same indifference as older folks. With both orders of mind we have to deal. It is well to explain to children the ordinance of the Lord's Supper, for this shows forth the death of Christ in symbol. I regret that children do not oftener see this ordinance. Baptism and the Lord's Supper should both be placed in view of the rising generation, that they may then ask us, "What mean ye by this?" Now, the Lord's Supper is a perennial gospel sermon, and it turns mainly upon the sacrifice for sin. You may banish the doctrine of the atonement from the pulpit, but it will always live in the church through the Lord's Supper. You cannot explain that broken bread and that cup filled with the fruit of the vine, without reference to our Lord's atoning death. You cannot explain "the communion of the body of Christ" without bringing in, in some form or other, the death of Jesus in our place and stead. Let your little ones, then, see the Lord's Supper, and let them be told most clearly what it sets forth. And if not the Lord's Supper—for that is not the thing itself, but only the shadow of the glorious fact—dwell much and often in their presence upon the sufferings and death of our Redeemer. Let them think of Gethsemane, and Gabbatha, and Golgotha, and let them learn to sing in plaintive tones of him who laid down his life for us. Tell them who it was that suffered, and why. Yes, though the hymn is hardly to my taste in some of its expressions, I would have the children sing—

> "There is a green hill far away,
>   Without a city wall."

And I would have them learn such lines as these:

> "He knew how wicked we had been,
>   And knew that God must punish sin;
> So out of pity Jesus said,
>   He'd bear the punishment instead."

And when attention is excited upon the best of themes, let us be ready to explain the great transaction by which God is just, and yet sinners are justified. Children can well understand the doctrine of the expiatory sacrifice; it was meant to be a gospel for the youngest. The gospel of substitution is a simplicity, though it is a mystery. We ought not to be content until our little ones know and trust in their finished sacrifice. This is essential knowledge, and the key to all other spiritual teaching. May our dear children know the cross, and they will have begun well. With all their gettings may they get an understanding of this, and they will have the foundation rightly laid.

This will necessitate your teaching the child his need of a Saviour. You must not hold back from this needful task. Do not flatter the child with delusive rubbish about his nature being good and needing to be developed. Tell him he must be born again. Don't bolster him up with the fancy of his own innocence, but show him his sin. Mention the childish sins to which he is prone, and pray the Holy Spirit to work conviction in his heart and conscience. Deal with the young in much the same way as you would with the old. Be thorough and honest with them. Flimsy religion is neither good for young nor old. These boys and girls need pardon through the precious blood as surely as any of us. Do not hesitate to tell the child his ruin; he will not else desire the remedy. Tell him also of the punishment of sin, and warn him of its terror. Be tender, but be true. Do not hide from the youthful sinner the truth, however terrible it may be. Now that he has come to years of responsibility, if he believes not in Christ, it will go ill with him at the last great day. Set before him the judgment-seat, and remind him that he will have to give an account of things done in the body. Labour to arouse the conscience; and pray God the Holy Spirit to work by you till the heart becomes tender and the mind perceives the need of the great salvation.

Children need to learn the doctrine of the cross that they may find immediate salvation. I thank God that in our Sabbath-school we believe in the salvation of children as children. How very many has it been my joy to see of boys and girls who have come forward to confess their faith in Christ! and I again wish to say that the best converts, the clearest converts, the most intelligent converts we have ever had have been the young ones; and, instead of there being any deficiency in their knowledge of the Word of God, and the doctrines of grace, we have usually found them to have a very delightful acquaintance with the great cardinal truths of Christ. Many of these dear children have been able to speak of the things of God with great pleasure of heart, and force of understanding. Go on, dear teachers, and believe that God will save your children. Be not content to sow principles in their minds which may possibly develop in after years; but be working for immediate conversion. Expect fruit in your children while they are children. Pray for them that they may not run into the world and fall into the evils of outward sin, and then come back with broken bones to the Good Shepherd; but that they may by God's rich grace be kept from the paths of the destroyer, and grow up in the fold of Christ, first as lambs of his flock, and then as sheep of his hand.

One thing I am sure of, and that is, that if we teach the children the doctrine of the atonement in the most unmistakable terms, we shall be doing ourselves good. I sometimes hope that God will revive his church and restore her to her ancient faith by a gracious work among children. If he would bring into our churches a large influx of young people, how it would tend to quicken the sluggish blood of the supine and sleepy! Child Christians tend to keep the house alive. Oh, for more of them! If the Lord will but help us to teach the children we shall be teaching ourselves. There is no way of learning like teaching, and you do not know a thing till you can teach it to another. You do not thoroughly know any truth till you can put it before a child so that he can see it. In trying to make a little child understand the doctrine of the atonement you will get clearer views of it yourselves, and there-fore I commend the holy exercise to you.

What a mercy it will be if our children are thoroughly grounded in the doctrine of redemption by Christ! If they are warned against the false gospels of this evil age, and if they are taught to rest on the eternal rock of Christ's finished work, we may hope to have a genera-tion following us which will maintain the faith, and will be better than their fathers. Your Sunday-schools are admirable; but what is their purpose if you do not teach the gospel in them? You get children together and keep them quiet for an hour-and-a-half, and then send them home; but what is the good of it? It may bring some quiet to their fathers and mothers, and that is, perhaps, why they send them to the school; but all the real good lies in what is taught the children. The most fundamental truth should be made most prominent; and what is this but the cross? Some talk to chil-dren about being good boys and girls, and so on; that is to say, they preach the law to the children, though they would preach the gospel to grown-up people! Is this honest? Is this wise? Children need the gospel, the whole gospel, the unadulterated gospel; they ought to have it, and if they are taught of the Spirit of God they are as capable of receiving it as persons of ripe years. Teach the little ones that Jesus died, the just for the unjust, to bring us to God. Very, very confidently do I leave this work in the hands of the teachers of this school. I never knew a nobler body of Christian men and women; for they are as earnest in their attachment to the old gospel as they are eager for the winning of souls. Be encouraged, my brothers and sisters: the God who has saved so many of your children is going to save very many more of them, and we shall have great joy in this Tabernacle as we see hundreds brought to Christ. God grant it, for his name's sake! Amen.

10 Young Man, Is This for You?

"And it came to pass the day after, that he went into a city called Nain; and many of his disciples went with him, and much people. Now when he came nigh to the gate of the city, behold, there was a dead man carried out, the only son of his mother, and she was a widow: and much people of the city was with her. And when the Lord saw her, he had compassion on her, and said unto her, Weep not. And he came and touched the bier: and they that bare him stood still. And he said, Young man, I say unto thee, Arise. And he that was dead sat up, and began to speak. And he delivered him to his mother. And there came a fear on all: and they glorified God, saying, That a great prophet is risen up among us; and, That God hath visited his people. And this rumour of him went forth throughout all Judæa, and throughout all the region round about."—Luke vii. 11—17.

BEHOLD, dear brethren, the overflowing, ever-flowing power of our Lord Jesus Christ. He had wrought a great work upon the centurion's servant, and now, only a day after, he raises the dead. "It came to pass the day after, that he went into a city called Nain." Day unto day uttereth speech concerning his deeds of goodness. Did he save your friend yesterday? His fulness is the same; if you seek him, his love and grace will flow to you to-day. He blesses this day, and he blesses the day after. Never is our divine Lord compelled to pause until he has recruited his resources; but virtue goeth out of him for ever. These thousands of years have not diminished the aboundings of his power to bless.

Behold, also, the readiness and naturalness of the outgoings of his life-giving power. Our Saviour was journeying, and he works miracles while on the road: "He went into a city called Nain." It was incidentally, some would say accidentally, that he met the funeral procession; but at once he restored to life this dead young man. Our blessed Lord was not standing still, as one professionally called in; he does not seem to have come to Nain at any one's request for the display of his love; but he was passing through the gate into the city, for some reason which is not recorded. See, my brethren, how the Lord Jesus is always ready to save! He healed the woman who touched him in the throng when he was on the road to quite another person's house. The mere spillings and droppings of the Lord's cup of grace are marvellous. Here he gives life to the dead when he is *en route;* he scatters his mercy by the roadside, and anywhere and everywhere his paths drop fatness. No time, no place, can find Jesus

111

unwilling or unable. When Baal is on a journey, or sleepeth, his deluded worshippers cannot hope for his help; but when Jesus journeys or sleeps, a word will find him ready to conquer death, or quell the tempest.

It was a remarkable incident, this meeting of the two processions at the gates of Nain. If some one with a fine imagination could picture it, what an opportunity he would have for developing his poetical genius! I venture on no such effort. Yonder a procession descends from the city. Our spiritual eyes see death upon the pale horse coming forth from the city gate with great exultation. He has taken another captive. Upon that bier behold the spoils of the dread conqueror! Mourners by their tears confess the victory of death. Like a general riding in triumph to the Roman capitol, death bears his spoils to the tomb. What shall hinder him? Suddenly the procession is arrested by another: a company of disciples and much people are coming up the hill. We need not look at the company, but we may fix our eyes upon one who stands in the centre, a man in whom lowliness was always evident, and yet majesty was never wanting. It is the living Lord, even he who only hath immortality, and in him death has now met his destroyer. The battle is short and decisive; no blows are struck, for death has already done his utmost. With a finger the chariot of death is arrested; with a word the spoil is taken from the mighty, and the lawful captive is delivered. Death flies defeated from the gates of the city, while Tabor and Hermon, which both looked down upon the scene, rejoice in the name of the Lord. This was a rehearsal upon a small scale of that which shall happen by-and-by, when those who are in their graves shall hear the voice of the Son of God and live: then shall the last enemy be destroyed. Only let death come into contact with him who is our life, and it is compelled to relax its hold, whatever may be the spoil which it has captured. Soon shall our Lord come in his glory, and then before the gates of the New Jerusalem we shall see the miracle at the gates of Nain multiplied a myriad times.

Thus, you see, our subject would naturally conduct us to the doctrine of the resurrection of the dead, which is one of the foundation stones of our most holy faith. That grand truth I have often declared to you, and will do so again and again; but at this time I have selected my text for a very practical purpose, which concerns the souls of some for whom I am greatly anxious. The narrative before us records a fact, a literal fact, but the record may be used for spiritual instruction. All our Lord's miracles were intended to be parables: they were intended to instruct as well as to impress: they are sermons to the eye, just as his spoken discourses were sermons to the ear. We see here how Jesus can deal with spiritual death; and how he can impart spiritual life at his pleasure. Oh, that we may see this done this morning in the midst of this great assembly!

I. I shall ask you first, dear friends, to reflect that THE SPIRITUALLY DEAD CAUSE GREAT GRIEF TO THEIR GRACIOUS FRIENDS. If an ungodly man is favoured to have Christian relatives, he causes them much anxiety. As a natural fact, this dead young man, who was being carried out to his burial, caused his mother's heart to burst with

grief. She showed by her tears that her heart was overflowing with
sorrow. The Saviour said to her, "Weep not," because he saw how
deeply she was troubled. Many of my dear young friends may be
deeply thankful that they have friends who are grieving over them.
It is a sad thing that your conduct should grieve them; but it is a
hopeful circumstance for you that you have those around you who do
thus grieve. If all approved of your evil ways, you would, no doubt,
continue in them, and go speedily to destruction; but it is a blessing
that arresting voices do at least a little hinder you. Besides, it may
yet be that our Lord will listen to the silent oratory of your mother's
tears, and that this morning he may bless you for her sake. See how
the evangelist puts it : "When the Lord saw *her*, he had compassion
on *her*, and said unto *her*, Weep not." And then he said to the young
man, "Arise."

Many young persons who are in some respects amiable and hopeful,
nevertheless, being spiritually dead, *are causing great sorrow to those
who love them best.* It would perhaps be honest to say that they do not
intend to inflict all this sorrow; indeed, they think it quite unnecessary.
Yet they are a daily burden to those whom they love. Their conduct
is such that when it is thought over in the silence of their mother's
chamber, she cannot help but weep. Her son went with her to the
house of God when he was a boy, but now he finds his pleasure in a
very different quarter. Being beyond all control now, the young man
does not choose to go with his mother. She would not wish to deprive
him of his liberty, but she laments that he exercises that liberty so
unwisely; she mourns that he has not the inclination to hear the Word
of the Lord, and become a servant of his mother's God. She had
hoped that he would follow in his father's footsteps, and unite with
the people of God; but he takes quite the opposite course. She has
seen a good deal about him lately which has deepened her anxiety :
he is forming companionships and other connections which are sadly
harmful to him. He has a distaste for the quietude of home, and he
has been exhibiting to his mother a spirit which wounds her. It may
be that what he has said and done is not meant to be unkind; but it
is very grievous to the heart which watches over him so tenderly. She
sees a growing indifference to everything that is good, and an uncon-
cealed intention to see the vicious side of life. She knows a little, and
fears more, as to his present state, and she dreads that he will go
from one sin to another till he ruins himself for this life and the next.
O friends, it is to a gracious heart a very great grief to have an unconverted child ; and yet more so if that child is a mother's boy, her
only boy, and she a desolate woman, from whom her husband has been
snatched away. To see spiritual death rampant in one so dear is a
sore sorrow, which causes many a mother to mourn in secret, and pour
out her soul before God. Many a Hannah has become a woman of a
sorrowful spirit through her own child. How sad that he who should
have made her the gladdest among women has filled her life with
bitterness! Many a mother has had so to grieve over her son as almost
to cry, "Would God he had never been born !" It is so in thousands
of cases. If it be so in your case, dear friend, take home my words
to yourself, and reflect upon them.

The cause of grief lies here: *we mourn that they should be in such a case*. In the story before us the mother wept because her son was dead; and we sorrow because our young friends are spiritually dead. There is a life infinitely higher than the life which quickens our material bodies; and oh that all of you knew it! You, who are un-renewed, do not know anything about this true life. Oh, how we wish you did! It seems to us a dreadful thing that you should be dead to God, dead to Christ, dead to the Holy Spirit. It is sad, indeed, that you should be dead to those divine truths which are the delight and strength of our souls; dead to those holy motives which keep us back from evil, and spur us on to virtue; dead to those sacred joys which often bring us very near the gates of heaven. We cannot look at a dead man, and feel joy in him, whoever he may be: a corpse, however delicately dressed, is a sad sight. We cannot look upon you, ye poor dead souls, without crying out, " O God, shall it always be so? Shall not these dry bones live? Wilt thou not quicken them?" The apostle speaks of one who lived in pleasure, and he said of her, "She is dead while she liveth." Numbers of persons are dead in reference to all that is truest, and noblest, and most divine; and yet in other respects they are full of life and activity. Oh, to think that they should be dead to God, and yet so full of jollity and energy! Marvel not that we grieve about them.

We also mourn because we lose the help and comfort which they ought to bring us. This widowed mother no doubt mourned her boy, not only because he was dead, but because in him she had lost her earthly stay. She must have regarded him as the staff of her age, and the comfort of her loneliness. " She was a widow": I question if any-body but a widow understands the full sorrow of that word. We may put ourselves by sympathy into the position of one who has lost her other self, the partner of her life; but the tenderest sympathy cannot fully realize the actual cleavage of bereavement, and the desolation of love's loss. " She was a widow"—the sentence sounds like a knell. Still, if the sun of her life was gone, there was a star shining; she had a boy, a dear boy, who promised her great comfort. He would, no doubt, supply her necessities, and cheer her loneliness, and in him her husband would live again, and his name would remain among the living in Israel. She could lean on him as she went to the synagogue; she would have him to come home from his work at evening, and keep the little home together, and cheer her hearth. Alas! that star is swallowed up in the darkness. He is dead, and to-day he is borne to the cemetery. It is the same spiritually with us in reference to our unconverted friends. With regard to you that are dead in sin, we feel that we miss the aid and comfort which we ought to receive from you in our service of the living God. We want fresh labourers in all sorts of places—in our Sunday-school work, our mission among the masses, and in all manner of service for the Lord we love! Ours is a gigantic burden, and we long for our sons to put their shoulders to it. We did look forward to see you grow up in the fear of God, and stand side by side with us in the great warfare against evil, and in holy labour for the Lord Jesus; but you cannot help us, for you are yourselves on the wrong side. Alas, alas! you hinder us by causing the world to say, "See how those young men are acting!" We have to spend thought, and prayer, and effort over you which might usefully have gone forth for others. Our care for yonder great dark world which lies all around us is very pressing, but you do not share it with us: men are perishing from lack of knowledge, and you do not help us in endeavouring to enlighten them.

A further grief is that we can have no fellowship with them. The mother at Nain could have no communion with her dear son now that he was dead, for the dead know not anything. He can never speak to her, nor she to him, for he is on the bier, "a dead man carried out." O my friends, certain of you have dear ones whom you love, and they love you; but they cannot hold any spiritual communion with you, nor you with them. You never bow the knee together in private prayer, nor mingle heart with heart in the appeal of faith to God as to the cares which prowl around your home. O young man, when your mother's heart leaps for joy because of the love of Christ shed abroad in her soul, you cannot understand her joy. Her feelings are a mystery to you. If you are a dutiful son, you do not say anything disrespectful about her religion; but yet you cannot sympathize in its sorrows or its joys. Between your mother and you there is upon the best things a gulf as wide as if you were actually dead on the bier, and she stood weeping over your corpse. I remember, in the hour of overwhelming anguish when I feared that my beloved wife was about to be taken from me, how I was comforted by the loving prayers of my two dear sons: we had communion not only in our grief, but in our confidence in the living God. We knelt together and poured out our hearts unto God, and we were comforted. How I blessed God that I had in my children such sweet support! But suppose they had been ungodly young men! I should have looked in vain for holy fellowship, and for aid at the throne of grace. Alas! in many a household the mother cannot have communion with her own son or daughter on that point which is most vital and enduring, because they are spiritually dead, while she has been quickened into newness of life by the Holy Spirit.

Moreover, *spiritual death soon produces manifest causes for sorrow.* In the narrative before us the time had come when her son's body must be buried. She could not wish to have that dead form longer in the home with her. It is a token to us of the terrible power of death, that it conquers love with regard to the body. Abraham loved his Sarah; but after a while he had to say to the sons of Heth, "Give me a possession of a burying-place with you, that I may bury my dead out of my sight." It happens in some mournful cases that character becomes so bad that no comfort in life can be enjoyed while the erring one is within the home circle. We have known parents who have felt that they could not have their son at home, so drunken, so debauched had he become. Not always wisely, yet sometimes almost of necessity, the plan has been tried of sending the incorrigible youth to a distant colony, in the hope that when removed from pernicious influences he might do better. How seldom so deplorable an experiment succeeds! I have known mothers who could not think of their sons without feeling pangs far more bitter than those they endured at their birth. Woe, woe to him who causes such heart-break!

What an awful thing it is when love's best hopes gradually die down into despair, and loving desires at last put on mourning, and turn from prayers of hope to tears of regret! Words of admonition call forth such passion and blasphemy that prudence almost silences them. Then have we before us the dead young man carried out to his grave. A sorrowful voice sobs out, "He is given unto idols, let him alone." Am I addressing one whose life is now preying upon the tender heart of her that brought him forth? Do I speak to one whose outward conduct has at last become so avowedly wicked that he is a daily death to those who gave him life? O young man, can you bear to think of this? Are you turned to stone? I cannot yet believe that you contemplate your parents' heart-break without bitter feelings. God forbid that you should!

We also mourn because of the future of men dead in sin. This mother, whose son had already gone so far in death that he must be buried out of sight, had the further knowledge that something worse would befall him in the sepulchre to which he was being carried. It was impossible for her to think calmly of the corruption which surely follows at the heels of death. When we think of what will become of you who refuse the Lord Christ we are appalled. "After death the judgment." We could more readily go into details as to a putrid corpse than we could survey the state of a soul lost for ever. We dare not linger at the mouth of hell; but we are forced to remind you that there is a place "where their worm dieth not, and the fire is not quenched." There is a place where those must abide who are driven from the presence of the Lord, and from the glory of his power. It is an unendurable thought, that you should be "cast into the lake of fire, which is the second death." I do not wonder that those who are not honest with you are afraid to tell you so, and that you try yourself to doubt it; but with the Bible in your hand, and a conscience in your bosom, you cannot but fear the worst if you remain apart from Jesus and the life he freely gives. If you continue as you are, and persevere in your sin and unbelief to the end of life, there is no help for it but that you must be condemned in the day of judgment. The most solemn declarations of the Word of God assure you that "he that believeth not shall be damned." It is heart-breaking work to think that this should be the case with any one of you. You prattled at your mother's knee, and kissed her cheek with rapturous love; why, then, will you be divided from her for ever? Your father hoped that you would take his place in the church of God; how is it that you do not even care to follow him to heaven? Remember, the day comes when "one shall be taken, and the other left." Do you renounce all hope of being with your wife, your sister, your mother, at the right hand of God? You cannot wish them to go down to hell with you; have you no desire to go to heaven with them? "Come, ye blessed," will be the voice of Jesus to those who imitated their gracious Saviour; and "Depart from me, ye cursed, into everlasting fire, prepared for the devil and his angels," must be the sentence upon all who refuse to be made like the Lord. Why will you take your part and lot with accursed ones?

I do not know whether you find it easy to hear me this morning.

I find it very hard to speak to you, because my lips are not able to express my heart's feelings. Oh that I had the forceful utterance of an Isaiah, or the passionate lamentations of a Jeremiah, with which to arouse your affections and your fears! Still, the Holy Spirit can use even me, and I beseech him so to do. It is enough. I am sure you see that the spiritually dead cause great grief to those of their family who are spiritually alive.

II. Now let me cheer you while I introduce the second head of my discourse, which is this: FOR SUCH GRIEF THERE IS ONLY ONE HELPER: BUT THERE IS A HELPER. This young man is taken out to be buried; but *our Lord Jesus Christ met the funeral procession.* Carefully note the "coincidences," as sceptics call them, but as we call them "providences" of Scripture." This is a fine subject for another time. Take this one case. How came it that the young man died just then? How came it that this exact hour was selected for his burial? Perhaps because it was evening; but even that might not fix the precise moment. Why did the Saviour that day arrange to travel five-and-twenty miles, so as to arrive at Nain in the evening? How came it to pass that he happened just then to be coming from a quarter which naturally led him to enter at that particular gate from which the dead would be borne? See, he ascends the hill to the little city at the same moment when the head of the procession is coming out of the gate! He meets the dead man before the place of sepulture is reached. A little later and he would have been buried; a little earlier and he would have been at home lying in the darkened room, and no one might have called the Lord's attention to him. The Lord knows how to arrange all things; his forecasts are true to the tick of the clock. I hope some great purpose is to be fulfilled this morning. I do not know why you, my friend, came in here on a day when I am discoursing on this particular subject. You did not think to come, perhaps, but here you are. And Jesus has come here too; he has come here on purpose to meet you, and quicken you to newness of life. There is no chance about it, eternal decrees have arranged it all, and we shall soon see that it is so. You being spiritually dead are met by him in whom is life eternal.

The blessed Saviour saw all at a glance. Out of that procession he singled out the chief mourner, and read her inmost heart. He was always tender to mothers. He fixed his eye on that widow; for he knew that she was such, without being informed of the fact. The dead man is her only son: he perceives all the details, and feels them all intensely. O young man, Jesus knows all about you. Nothing is hid from his infinite mind. Your mother's heart and yours are both open to him. Jesus, who is invisibly present this morning, fixes his eyes on you at this moment. He has seen the tears of those who have wept for you. He sees that some of them despair of you, and are in their great grief acting like mourners at your funeral.

Jesus saw it all, and, what was more, *entered into it all.* Oh, how we ought to love our Lord that he takes such notice of our griefs, and especially our spiritual griefs about the souls of others! You, dear teacher, want your class saved: Jesus sympathizes with you. You, dear friend, have been very earnest to win souls. Know that in all this you are workers together with God. Jesus knows all about our travail of soul, and he is at one with us therein. Our travail is only his own travail rehearsed in us, according to our humble measure. When Jesus enters into our work it cannot fail. Enter, O Lord, into my work at this hour, I pray thee, and bless this feeble word to my hearers! I know that hundreds of believers are saying, "Amen." How this cheers me!

Our Lord proved how he entered into the sorrowful state of things by first saying to the widow, "Weep not." At this moment he says to you who are praying and agonizing for souls, "Do not despair! Sorrow not as those who are without hope! I mean to bless you. You shall yet rejoice over life given to the dead." Let us take heart and dismiss all unbelieving fear.

Our Lord then went to the bier, and just laid his finger upon it, and *they that bare it stood still of their own accord.* Our Lord has a way of making bearers stand still without a word. Perhaps to-day yonder young man is being carried further into sin by the four bearers of his natural passions, his infidelity, his bad company, and his love of strong drink. It may be that pleasure and pride, wilfulness and wickedness are bearing the four corners of the bier; but our Lord can, by his mysterious power, make the bearers stand still. Evil influences have become powerless, the man knows not how.

When they stood quite still, *there was a hush.* The disciples stood around the Lord, the mourners surrounded the widow, and the two crowds faced each other. There was a little space, and Jesus and the dead man were in the centre. The widow pushed away her veil, and gazing through her tears wondered what was coming. The Jews who came out of the city halted as the bearers had done. Hush! Hush! What will HE do? In that deep silence the Lord heard the unspoken prayers of that widow woman. I doubt not that her soul began to whisper, half in hope, and half in fear—"Oh, that he would raise my son!" At any rate, Jesus heard the flutter of the wings of desire if not of faith. Surely her eyes were speaking as she gazed on Jesus, who had so suddenly appeared. Here let us be as quiet as the scene before us. Let us be hushed for a minute, and pray God to raise dead souls at this time. (Here followed a pause, much silent prayer, and many tears.)

III. That hush was not long, for speedily the Great Quickener entered upon his gracious work. This is our third point: JESUS IS ABLE TO WORK THE MIRACLE OF LIFE-GIVING. Jesus Christ has life in himself, and he quickeneth whom he will (John v. 21). Such life is there in him that "he that liveth and believeth in him, though he were dead, yet shall he live." Our blessed Lord immediately went up to the bier. What lay before him? It was a corpse. *He could derive no aid from that lifeless form.* The spectators were sure that he was dead, for they were carrying him out to bury him. No deception was possible, for his own mother believed him dead, and you may be sure that if there had been a spark of life in him she would not have given him up to the jaws of the grave. There was then no hope—no hope from the dead man, no hope from any one in the crowd either of bearers or of disciples. They were all powerless alike. Even so, you, O sinner, cannot save yourself, neither can any of us, or all of us save you.

There is no help for you, dead sinner, beneath yon skies; no help in yourself or in those who love you best. But, lo, the Lord hath laid help on one that is mighty. If Jesus wants the least help you cannot render it, for you are dead in sins. There you lie, dead on the bier, and nothing but the sovereign power of divine omnipotence can put heavenly life into you. Your help must come from above.

While the bier stood still, Jesus spoke to the dead young man, *spoke to him personally:* "Young man, I say unto thee, Arise." O Master, personally speak to some young man this morning; or, if thou wilt, speak to the old, or speak to a woman; but speak the word home to them. We mind not where the Lord's voice may fall. Oh that it would now call those around me, for I feel that there are dead ones all over the building! I stand with biers all about me, and dead ones on them. Lord Jesus, art thou not here? What is wanted is thy personal call. Speak, Lord, we beseech thee!

"Young man," said he, "arise;" and *he spake as if the man had been alive.* This is the gospel way. He did not wait till he saw signs of life before he bade him rise; but to the dead man he said, "Arise." This is the model of gospel preaching: in the name of the Lord Jesus, his commissioned servants speak to the dead as if they were alive. Some of my brethren cavil at this, and say that it is inconsistent and foolish; but all through the New Testament it is even so. There we read, "Arise from the dead, and Christ shall give thee light." I do not attempt to justify it; it is more than enough for me that so I read the Word of God. We are to bid men believe on the Lord Jesus Christ, even though we know that they are dead in sin, and that faith is the work of the Spirit of God. Our faith enables us in God's name to command dead men to live, and they do live. We bid unbelieving man believe in Jesus, and power goes with the Word, and God's elect do believe. It is by this word of faith which we preach that the voice of Jesus sounds out to men. The young man who could not rise, for he was dead, nevertheless did rise when Jesus bade him. Even so, when the Lord speaks by his servants the gospel command, "Believe and live," is obeyed, and men live.

But the Saviour, you observe, *spoke with his own authority*—"Young man, *I say unto thee*, Arise." Neither Elijah nor Elisha could thus have spoken; but he who spoke thus was very God of very God. Though veiled in human flesh, and clothed in lowliness, he was that same God who said, "Let there be light, and there was light." If any of us are able by faith to say, "Young man, Arise," we can only say it in *his* name—we have no authority but what we derive from *him*. Young man, the voice of Jesus can do what your mother cannot. How often has her sweet voice wooed you to come to Jesus, but wooed in vain! Oh, that the Lord Jesus would inwardly speak to you! Oh, that he would say, "Young man, Arise." I trust that while I am speaking the Lord is silently speaking in your hearts by his Holy Spirit. I feel sure that it is even so. If so, within you a gentle movement of the Spirit is inclining you to repent and yield your heart to Jesus. This shall be a blessed day to the spiritually dead young

man, if now he accepts his Saviour, and yields himself **up to be**
renewed by grace. No, my poor brother, they shall not bury you!
I know you have been very bad, and they may well despair of you;
but while Jesus lives we cannot give you up.

The miracle was wrought straightway : for this young man, to the
astonishment of all about him, sat up. His was a desperate case, but
death was conquered, for he sat up. He had been called back from
the innermost dungeon of death, even from the grave's mouth; but
he sat up when Jesus called him. It did not take a month, nor a
week, nor an hour, nay, not even five minutes. Jesus said, "Young
man, Arise." And he that was dead sat up, and began to speak." In
an instant the Lord can save a sinner. Ere the words I speak can
have more than entered your ear, the divine flash which gives you
eternal life can have penetrated your breast, and you shall be a new
creature in Jesus Christ, beginning to live in newness of life from this
hour, no more to feel spiritually dead, or to return to your old corruption.
New life, new feeling, new love, new hopes, new company shall be
yours, because you have passed from death unto life. Pray God that
it may be so, for he will hear us.

IV. Our time has gone, and although we have a wide subject we
may not linger. I must close by noticing that THIS WILL PRODUCE
VERY GREAT RESULTS. To give life to the dead is no little matter.

The great result was manifest, first, in the young man. Would you
like to see him as he was? Might I venture to draw back the sheet
from his face? See there what death has done. He was a fine young
man. To his mother's eye he was the mirror of manhood! What
a pallor is on that face! How sunken are the eyes! You are feeling
sad. I see you cannot bear the sight. Come, look into this grave,
where corruption has gone further in its work. Cover him up! We
cannot bear to look at the decaying body! But when Jesus Christ
has said, "Arise," what a change takes place! Now you may look
at him. His blue eye has the light of heaven in it; his lips are
coral red with life; his brow is fair and full of thought. Look at his
healthy complexion, in which the rose and the lily sweetly contend for
mastery. What a fresh look there is about him, as of the dew of
the morning! He has been dead, but he lives, and no trace of death
is on him. While you are looking at him he begins to speak.
What music for his mother's ear! What did he say? Why, that I
cannot tell you. Speak yourself as a newly-quickened one, and then
I shall hear what you say. I know what *I* said. I think the first
word I said when I was quickened was, "Hallelujah." Afterwards,
I went home to my mother, and told her that the Lord had met with
me. No words are given here. It does not quite matter what those
words are, for any words proved him to be alive. If you know the
Lord, I believe you will speak of heavenly things. I do not believe
that our Lord Jesus has a dumb child in his house : they all speak *to*
him, and most of them speak *of* him. The new birth reveals itself in
confession of Christ, and praise of Christ. I warrant you, that his
mother, when she heard him speak, did not criticize what he said.
She did not say, "That sentence is ungrammatical." She was too
glad to hear him speak at all, that she did not examine all the

expressions which he used. Newly-saved souls often talk in a way which after years and experience will not justify. You often hear it said of a revival meeting, that there was a good deal of excitement, and certain young converts talked absurdly. That is very likely: but if genuine grace was in their souls, and they bore witness to the Lord Jesus, I for one would not criticize them very severely. Be glad if you can see any proof that they are born again, and mark well their future lives. To the young man himself a new life had begun—life from among the dead.

A new life also had begun in reference to *his mother*. What a great result for her was the raising of her dead son! Henceforth he would be doubly dear. Jesus helped him down from the bier, and delivered him to his mother. We have not the words he used; but we are sure that he made the presentation most gracefully, giving back the son to the mother as one presents a choice gift. With a majestic delight which always goes with his condescending benevolence, he looked on that happy woman, and his glance was brighter to her than the light of the morning, as he said to her, "Receive thy son." The thrill of her heart was such as she would never forget. Observe carefully that our Lord, when he puts the new life into young men, does not want to take them away with him from the home where their first duty lies. Here and there one is called away to be an apostle or a missionary; but usually he wants them to go home to their friends, and bless their parents, and make their families happy and holy. He does not present the young man to the priest, but he delivers him to his mother. Do not say, "I am converted, and therefore I cannot go to business any more, or try to support my mother by my trade." That would prove that you were not converted at all. You may go for a missionary in a year or two's time if you are fitted for it; but you must not make a dash at a matter for which you are not prepared. For the present go home to your mother, and make your home happy, and charm your father's heart, and be a blessing to your brothers and sisters, and let them rejoice because "he was dead, and is alive again; he was lost, and is found."

What was the next result? Well, all the neighbours feared and glorified God. If yonder young man who last night was at the music-hall, and a few nights ago came home very nearly drunk; if that young man is born again, all around him will wonder at it. If that young man who has got himself out of a situation by gambling, or some other wrong-doing, is saved, we shall all feel that God is very near us. If that young man who has begun to associate with evil women, and to fall into other evils, is brought to be pure-minded and gracious, it will strike awe into those round about him. He has led many others astray, and if the Lord now leads him back it will make a great hubbub, and men will enquire as to the reason of the change, and will see that there is a power in religion after all. Conversions are miracles which never cease. These prodigies of power in the moral world are quite as remarkable as prodigies in the material world. We want conversion, so practical, so real, so divine, that those who doubt will not be able to doubt, because they see in them the hand of God.

Finally, note that it not only surprised the neighbours and impressed them, but the rumour of it went everywhere. Who can tell? If a convert is made this morning, the result of that conversion may be felt for thousands of years, if the world stands so long; ay, it shall be felt when a thousand thousand years have passed away, even throughout eternity. Tremblingly have I dropped a smooth stone into the lake this morning. It has fallen from a feeble hand and from an earnest heart. Your tears have shown that the waters are stirred. I perceive the first circlet upon the surface. Other and wider circles will follow as the sermon is spoken of and read. When you go home and tell what God has done for your soul, there will be a wider ring; and if it should happen that the Lord should open the mouth of one of this morning's converts to preach his word, then no one can tell how wide the circle will become. Ring upon ring will the word spread itself, until the shoreless ocean of eternity shall feel the influence of this morning's word. No, I am not dreaming. According to our faith so shall it be. Grace this day bestowed by the Lord upon one single soul may affect the whole mass of humanity. God grant his blessing, even life for evermore. Pray much for a blessing. My dear friends, I beseech you, for Jesus Christ's sake, pray much for me. Amen.

11 Young Man! A Prayer for You

"And Elisha prayed, and said, Lord, I pray thee, open his eyes, that he may see. And the Lord opened the eyes of the young man; and he saw: and, behold, the mountain was full of horses and chariots of fire round about Elisha."—2 Kings vi. 17.

THIS young man waited upon a prophet: he could not have had a more instructive occupation; yet his eyes needed to be opened. He was well disposed towards good things, for the tone of his language to his master shows that he was heartily at one with him; but his eyes were not yet half opened. Being in great alarm for his master's safety, he ran to him to warn him: good servants should be their master's best friends. In return, his believing master prays for him. If we desire the good of our servants, our children, and our friends, let us take care that we make supplication for them. All that we can do for them at our best is to give them secondary blessings; but if we pray to God for them, they will receive the best of gifts from him who sends down in his mercy nothing but good gifts and perfect gifts. When we have come to the end of our teaching, and example, and persuasion, let us hand our young friends over to the Lord, who works effectually unto eternal salvation.

Elisha's petition for this young man was, "O Lord, I pray thee, open his eyes, that he may see!" The young man was at that time in the peculiar condition of seeing, and yet not seeing. He saw the enemy surrounding the city, but not the greater host of the Lord's angels who protected the man of God. Looking over the little walls of Dothan, he observed all the country round about to be occupied by the horses and chariots of the king of Syria; and he cried, "Alas, my master! how shall we do?" He could see the danger, but he could not see the deliverance; and therefore the prophet lifted up his heart to heaven, and said, "O Lord, I pray thee, open his eyes, that he may see!" Elisha reckons his servant's natural sight as not seeing, and regards the vision which detects the invisible as the only true sight. Perhaps I am addressing some, at this time, who are very friendly to the cause of God, and are even connected with it by relationship or occupation; they cheerfully lend a hand at any time in holy service so far as they can, and they wish prosperity to the cause of true religion. Yet their eyes have not been opened to see spiritual things; or, at least, not sufficiently opened to see the gracious and divine side of them. They see enough to perceive that they are in danger from a great enemy. They perceive that it is no easy thing to fight the battle of life: in the prospect of it they cry, "How shall we do?" They perceive that it is a difficult thing for a man to stand up for holiness, for truth, for integrity, for purity, and to maintain a gracious character throughout the whole of life. They seem to themselves to be environed with opposing forces in their business, in their temperament, in their companionships, and perhaps in their families. As for the cause of godliness, it seems hemmed in by adversaries; and they ask—What is to be done? Is not the matter desperate? Might it not be as well to surrender at once? For any such timid one I would present to God the prayer of Elisha: " O Lord, I pray thee, open his eyes, that he may see!" Oh, that the prayer might be answered at this hour!

Very briefly, I shall speak, first, upon *our prayer;* secondly, upon *our reason* for offering such a petition; and thirdly, upon *our hope;* for we trust that, if our prayer is answered, the person whose eyes are opened will behold a vision which will bless him beyond anything he has ever dreamed of.

I. First, then, OUR PRAYER: "Lord, I pray thee, open the eyes of the young man, that he may see!" This petition bears many senses. I will mention a few only.

For certain of our friends we pray that their eyes may be opened *to see the enemy of their souls under the many disguises which he assumes.* We fear that many are ignorant of his devices. Young men, especially, are too apt to mistake the great enemy for a friend. They believe his false and flattering words, and are seduced to ruin. He holds forth to them the sparkling cup; but in its beaded bubbles death is lurking. He talks of "pleasure"; but in the lusts of the flesh the pleasure is a shadow, and misery is the substance. He wears the mask of prudence, and admonishes young men to "mind the main chance", and leave religion till they have made their fortunes; but that gain which comes of thrusting God aside will prove to be an everlasting loss. The devil as a serpent does more mischief than as a roaring lion. If we had to meet the devil, and knew him to be what he is, we might far more easily conquer him; but we have to deal with him disguised as an angel of light, and here is the need of a hundred eyes, each one of them opened by God, that we may see. Even worse than this is the fact that, at times, he does not meet us at all, but he undermines our path; he digs pits for our feet; he shoots his arrows from afar, or sends forth a pestilence which walks in darkness. Then have we need of a better sight than nature gives. I would pray for the young man who is just leaving home to go into the world, " O Lord, open the eyes of the young man, that he may see!" May he be able to detect the falsehood which may hide itself beneath the truth, the meanness which may wrap itself about with pride, the folly which may robe itself in learning, the sin which may dress itself in the raiment of pleasure! I would not have you taken, like birds, in a snare. I would not have the youth led, like a bullock to the shambles, by the hand of temptation. Let us breathe such a prayer as that of Elisha for each person in this place who is beginning life. God grant that his eyes may be opened to see sin as sin, and to see that evil never can be good, and a lie never can be true, and rebellion against our God can never be the way to happiness!

We want men's eyes to be opened *to see God as everywhere, observing all things*. What an opening of the eyes this would be to many! It is a sad but true saying, that God may be seen everywhere, but that the most of men see him nowhere. He is blind indeed who cannot see HIM to whom the sun owes its light. Until our eyes are opened, we rise in the morning, and we fall asleep at night, and we have not seen God all day, although he has been every moment around us and within us. We live from the first day of January to the last day of December, and while the Lord never ceases to see us, we do not even begin to see him till, by a miracle of grace, he opens our eyes. We dwell in a wonderful world which the great Creator has made, and filled with his own handiwork, and cheered with his own presence, and yet we do not see him: indeed, there are some so blind as to assert that there is no Creator, and that they cannot perceive any evidence that a supremely wise and mighty Creator exists. Oh, that the Lord Jesus would open the eyes of the wilfully blind! Oh, that you, also, who are blinded by forgetfulness rather than by error, may be made to cry with Hagar, "Thou God seest me"; and with Job, "Now mine eye seeth thee"! If God will graciously convince men of his own divine presence, what a benediction it will be to them, especially to the young in commencing life! A clear perception that the Lord observes all that we do will be a very useful protection in the hour of temptation. When we remember the divine eye, we shall cry, like Joseph, "How can I do this great wickedness, and sin against God?" To see yourself is well; but to see God is better. Let us pray, "O Lord, open the young man's eyes, that he may see THEE!"

When a man begins to see his great enemy, and his best Friend, we may next pray, Lord, open his eyes *to see the way of salvation through the appointed Saviour*. There is no seeing the Lord Jesus but by his own light. We look *to* him with a look which comes *from* him. I have tried to explain salvation to people many a time, in simple words and figures; but there is a great deal more wanted than an explanation. It is right to be very plain; but more is needed than a clear statement. No matter how bright the candle, a blind man sees none the better. I continually pray, "Lord, open my mouth"; but I perceive that I must also pray, "Lord, open men's eyes!" Until God opens a man's eyes, he will not see what faith means, nor what atonement means, nor what regeneration means. That which is plain as a pikestaff to a seeing man is invisible to the blind. "Believe, and live"; what can be plainer? Yet no man understands it till God gives grace to perceive his meaning. It is our duty, as preachers, to put the gospel as plainly as possible; but we cannot give a man spiritual understanding. We declare, in baldest and boldest terms, " Believe on the Lord Jesus Christ, and thou shalt be saved"; but men ask, like simpletons,

"What do you mean?" We cry, "Look unto Jesus, and live"; but when our explainings are over, we learn that they have mistaken our meaning, and are still looking to themselves, and turning their backs on the Lord Jesus. To believe, or trust, is no mystery, but the simplest of all simplicities; and for that very reason men cannot be persuaded to think that we mean what we say, or that God means what he says. We need to pray—Lord, open their eyes, that they may see; for seeing, they do not see; and hearing, they do not perceive!

Blessed be the Lord, how sweetly they do see it the moment their eyes are opened by his own omnipotent touch! Then they wonder that they did not see it before, and call themselves ten thousand fools for not perceiving what is so plain. Faith in the Lord Jesus is the veriest A B C of divine revelation: it belongs to the rudiments and elements of heavenly knowledge, and we are dolts indeed not to take it as we find it in the Word, and leave off mystifying ourselves over so plain a matter. Once let the miracle-working power of God open our eyes, and we see well enough; but till then we grope in the noon-day for that which is right before us. I hope, beloved fellow-Christians, that you are praying while I am speaking; praying, I mean, for those around you, and for all the blind souls that wander among the graves of earth: "Lord, open their eyes, that they may see!" He that made the eye can open it. Sin cannot so darken the mind but that God can pour light into it. If we cannot make men see, we can at least lead them to the Master Oculist, who can rectify their sight.

We should pray that our friends may have their eyes opened *to see all manner of spiritual truth.* These optics of ours can only see natural objects: that is all they are intended for. We should be very grateful that our eyes can see as much as they do see; but spiritual objects are not discernible by the eyes of the body, which are for material objects only. The things which pertain to the spiritual kingdom must be perceived by eyes of a spiritual sort, eyes opened by the Lord. God must give to us spiritual senses before we can discern spiritual things: let this never be forgotten. There are those sitting among us who cannot discern spiritual things, for they have not the needed faculties. Carnal men and carnal women see only carnal things. The flesh cannot grasp, perceive, or discern the things of the Spirit. We must become spiritual, and receive spiritual faculties, before we can perceive spiritual things; in a word, we must be "born again." "The natural man receiveth not the things of the Spirit of God: for they are foolishness unto him: neither can he know them, because they are spiritually discerned." Hence the need of the prayer, "Lord, open thou the eyes of the young man, that he may see!"

Already the horses and chariots of fire were round about Elisha; but his servant could not see one of them, because they were spiritual chariots and spiritual horses—angelic beings belonging to the purely spiritual domain; and as yet the youth had not entered the spiritual region, and had no eyes with which to see into it. When God had given him spiritual eyes, then there began to break upon his vision that strange sight—ethereal, aerial, nay, spiritual, but yet most real; that sight which revived his soul with the conviction that the prophet was safe, since the ministers of God, as flames of fire, flashed to and fro; and like an army, with horses and chariots, showed themselves strong for the defence of the servant of Jehovah. How surprised he was! How great his amazement! How content his mind! He and his master were mysteriously defended, beyond all fear of danger. O my hearers, as yet strangers to the things of God; if the Lord would open your eyes at once, you would be astonished indeed; for as yet you have no idea, you cannot have any idea, what the spiritual life is, nor what spiritual realities must be: neither can you have any true idea of them till you are quickened of the Lord. You may talk about spiritual subjects, and discuss them, and think yourselves theologians; but you resemble deaf persons criticizing music, and blind men describing pictures. You are not qualified even to express an opinion upon the matter till you are created anew in Christ Jesus, and brought within range of the spiritual and the heavenly. "Except a man be born again, he cannot see the kingdom of God." Let the prayer go up, then, from all enlightened hearts, for those who are not as yet walking in the light: "Lord, open the eyes of the young men, that they may see!"

We may expect a speedy answer. God does hear prayer. Who knows but that many sitting in this house may be surprised by the secret touch of the invisible Spirit, and all of a sudden may find themselves introduced into a new world? Elisha's prayer for this young man was not, and our prayer for others is not, that they may do something which they can do, that they may use some faculty which they already possess; but that a new sight may be granted to them, and that a new nature may be created within them, by a power altogether above and beyond themselves. We call in the hand of God. We ask the Lord to work a marvel. We would have you, dear friends, receive what no education can ever give you, what no graduation at any university can ever bestow upon you; we want you to obtain what no years of experience or of study can achieve; we want you to possess what no imitation of other people will gain for you; we want you to experience a change which only the Lord himself can work in you. We would have you pass from nature's darkness into God's marvellous light, from an awful blindness into a clear vision of things otherwise invisible. Register that prayer before the Lord, ye that are familiars in the courts of heaven! Present the prayer for children, and kinsfolk, and friends. Cry, "Lord, let them receive sight, through the gracious working of thy Holy Spirit!"

II. Secondly, let us set forth OUR REASON for praying such a prayer for those around us. On this occasion, I can truly say that I am praying much more than I am preaching. Whilst I am standing here before you, I am also bowing low before the Lord my God, and I am bearing upon my heart certain of you for whom I long in my heart, and have great heaviness of spirit. I am praying, in the secret of my soul, "Lord, open his eyes, that he may see!"

The first reason for our prayer is, because *we ourselves have been made to see.* Had this miracle of grace not taken place within us, we should have had no thought of prayer for you; but now our whole heart goes with the plea. Once we were as you are. Our eyes were blinded so that we saw neither our foes in all their terror, nor the glory of the Lord round about us. Like blind Samsons, we went through the weary drudgery of earth surrounded by our foes. At length a glimmering of the light fell upon us, like a lightning-flash, showing us our sin; and after we were thus illuminated we endured a great fight of afflictions. Without were fightings, within were fears. Our enemies were round about us, and we knew not what to do. But some man of God prayed for us, and one day our eyes were turned toward the hills from whence cometh all aid to terror-stricken men. The Lord was there, though we knew him not; but yet we looked to him and were enlightened, and our faces were not ashamed; for round about him the mountain was full of chariots and horses of fire. "For God, who commanded the light to shine out of darkness, hath shined in our hearts, to give the light of the knowledge of the glory of God in the face of Jesus Christ."

> " Lord, I was blind; I could not see
> In thy marred visage any grace;
> But now the beauty of thy face
> In radiant vision dawns on me."

What else but such a heavenly vision could have scattered all our guilty fear? What else could have given us peace in the midst of tumult? We did not quite understand how it was done, nor did the change come to all of us in the same way; but we can all say, "One thing I know, that whereas I was blind, now I see"; and since the prayers of others availed for us, we ought with double earnestness and hope to continue to plead for those who still have missed the glorious revelation. "Lord, open the eyes of the young man, that he may see!"

We call upon the Lord for this second reason, because *only by his power can men be made to see.* This we found in our own experience. In vain we struggled to behold the salvation of God; in vain we sought the help of godly people; no sight came to our souls, nor were the eyes of our understanding enlightened, until the Lord himself laved our eyes in the waters that go softly. Then we came seeing. And this we also discover when we try to lead others to the light. We speak to them of the glories we ourselves behold, and set before them the truth of God; but we cannot make them see. To bestow spiritual vision is as great a wonder as to make a world, and requires the same fiat of omnipotence. Only he who created the eye can give this second sight. "Since the world began was it not heard that any man opened the eyes of one that was born blind." What folly, then, to attempt the greater task of bestowing the sight of the heart! How vain the boast of those who attempt to invade God's prerogative, and imagine that human ordinances or observances can open blind eyes! Beloved, let us, after we have done our best to make the people see the glory of the gospel, ever fall back on the God of the gospel, and entreat him to do his own blessed work.

> " He comes, from thickest films of vice,
> To clear the mental ray;
> And on the eye-balls of the blind,
> To pour celestial day."

Do not try to hold up your tallow candles to reveal the chariots of fire, nor parade your vain philosophy, as if that could clear away the darkness of the soul. Leave room for God to work ; and, in a moment, at the touch of his finger, in response to the prayers of his people, the wondrous work shall be accomplished.

Most importunately do we pray when we see the people enquiring. The cry, " What shall we do ? " sends us to our knees ; for we know that what is necessary is, not something to be done, but something to be seen. And we feel persuaded that the Lord who awoke the desire in the hearts of the seekers, will surely, also, open their eyes to behold his glory. The very fact that we feel drawn to pray for them, is already a token to us that, ere long, the scales shall fall from their eyes ; and through their vision of the splendour and sufficiency of the provision that God hath made for those who trust in him, the name of the Lord will be greatly glorified. Therefore, with much expectancy, we again utter our prayer, " Lord, open their eyes, that they may see ! "

Another reason for this prayer is—*you are not aware of your own blindness.* You are trusting in yourselves that you can see well enough all you need to see. That young man, of whom I am thinking now, has no idea whatever that his eyes are stone blind to eternal things. He thinks himself a sharp and clever fellow ; and I do not deny that he is so, in his own line of things. I am glad that he has such quick faculties for this life. God bless him ; and may he prosper in his business, and in the enterprise upon which he is just entering ! May the good Lord be with him concerning the matter on which his heart is set ! But still, dear friend, I am rather afraid of your cleverness ; I am somewhat frightened at that keenness of yours, because I have seen sharp men cut themselves, and I have seen the self-reliant make miserable failures. Something is to be said for confidence in its proper place ; but self-congratulation is a proof of inward weakness, and forebodes a breakdown. If you are depending on an arm of flesh, at the very best you are resting on a broken reed ; you require a strength beyond your own to fight the moral and spiritual battle of life. Your self-reliance, in this case, is a piece of groundless self-conceit. Do you not remember one, of whom we read in this very Book of Kings, that, when he was forewarned of what he would yet do, he exclaimed, in astonishment, " Is thy servant a dog, that he should do this great thing ? " Hazael could not think himself capable of such crimes ; and yet he no sooner had the opportunity than he fell into the evil up to the very neck. He was dog enough to be cruel, for he was dog enough to fawn upon himself. You do not believe, young man, that you will ever be dishonest ; and yet that little gambling speculation of yours will lead to it. You cannot think that you will ever be godless ; and yet you are even now departing from the good old ways of your home, and making a jest of sacred things when in certain company. They that trust in themselves are storing up the fuel for a great fire of sin. The pride which lifts itself up will throw itself down. Because the fine young fellow does not know how blind he is, we therefore lament his blindness, and are the more earnest in bringing him to Jesus, that he may receive his sight. " Lord, open his eyes, that he may see ! "

Next, we pray this prayer, because we have reason to fear that

you are surrounded by those who will mislead you. We know the young
man well. He has newly come to London from that sober, orderly,
country home, and he has no notion of the snares which will be laid
for him by fowlers, male and female. Oh, you who have no experience, and little discretion, hear the voice of warning! Satan has
cunning servants about him, that hunt for the precious life with double
diligence. Our Lord Jesus has about him servants who too often
slumber; but the devil's servants are not slothful in their dreadful
business. You will find them waylay you in the streets without, and
press around you in the haunts of pleasure within. They are everywhere, and they leave no stone unturned that they may entrap the
unwary. And what if this blind young man is put down in the midst
of all these blood-suckers? They will devour him if they can : what
if he is left to be their victim? It is like turning out a sheep among
a pack of wolves. "Lord, open the eyes of the young man, that he
may see!"

We pray this prayer for some of you, because *you are going away from
those who have hitherto watched over you,* and this is a dangerous change
for you. Your mother—ah! we can never tell what a blessing a godly
mother is to a young man—your mother parts from you with great
anxiety. Will you ever forget her tender words? Our fathers are all
very well—God bless them!—and a father's godly influence and
earnest prayers are of untold value to his children; but the mothers are
worth two of them, mostly, as to the moral training and religious
bent of their sons and daughters. Well, I say, you are going right
away from your mother's holy influence, and from your father's
restraining admonitions. You will now have nobody to encourage
you in the right way. You will miss your sister's holy kiss, and your
grandmother's loving persuasions. You are going out of the hothouse into a night's frost : well may we pray concerning you, that you
may carry with you well-opened eyes, to see your way, and look before
you leap. The young man is now to walk alone: "Lord, open his
eyes, that he may see!" If he does not look before he leaps, he will
soon be in the ditch; and who shall pull him out?

Again, we pray this prayer with the more pleasure, because *you will
do so much good if your eyes are opened.* A blind man in the midst of
such a world as this, what can he do? He cannot help other travellers,
for he has to seek aid for himself. You wish to give rather than to
take, do you not? Some here have great abilities, and I want them
to use them aright. I am persuaded that I am speaking to young people
whom God has ordained to be of great service to their age. That
youth yonder does not as yet know what is in him. He is playing with
himself; he is making a fool of himself; he is throwing his pearls
before swine : he is wasting his strength. If the Lord should open
his eyes, he would see what he is doing. What a man he would make
if he were but right with God! Think of Saul of Tarsus, how he
harassed the church of Christ; but when the scales fell from his eyes,
the Lord had no better servant under heaven than that once-furious
persecutor. With both hands diligently he built up the church which
once he laboured to cast down. "The thing which has been is the
thing which shall be." Pray, therefore, O my brethren, for our young

men, who have sinned, that they may be restored; and for those who are as yet ignorant, that they may be enlightened; for the cause of God has need of these, and in these the church shall find her champions! Little know we the wealth of comfort for the faithful which may lie in one young life. Surely, we ought to pile on our prayers, and make our intercession flame like some great beacon-light for the rising youth of our time.

There is yet another reason, fetched from the other side of the case. We should pray for the blinded one, since *he may terribly sin if not soon made to see.* How capable of doing mischief is a man blinded by ignorance, by passion, by ambition, or by any other form of sin! Who knows the capacities for evil that lie within a single soul? That once bright spirit, Satan, when he first thought of raising revolt against the God of heaven; it was, perhaps, a single momentary flash of rebellious thought; but before long he had become proudly antagonistic to his Maker, and the dragon had drawn down with his tail a third part of the stars of heaven to quench them in the eternal night of endless wickedness. Then he came to this earth, and polluted Paradise, and seduced our first parents from their happy innocence, so that they became the progenitors of an unhappy race, steeped up to their lips in sin. That one first thought of ill, oh, how pregnant was it with innumerable evils! So, too, among ourselves. A boy, his mother's pride, to whom she looks forward as the honour of the family, may for a while appear to be everything that love can hope; but he falls into the hands of one of those tempters to unbelief who are so abundant in this great city. He is taught to pour ridicule upon his mother's piety, and soon he casts off the bands of his father's God. He forgets the sanctity of God's holy day, and forsakes the house of prayer; and then he learns the way to the houses of strange women, and to the palace of strong drink; and he plunges into one sin after another, till he is himself the leader of others down to the abyss. That boy, who used to kneel at his mother's knee, and say his childish prayer, and then stand up, and sing of Jesus and his love, was fondly regarded as one who would honour Jesus in his life; but see him now: he staggers home after midnight, vomiting oaths! He is foul both in soul and in body, and those who love him best are saddest at the sight of him. Dear friends, if we would not see our children or our friends running to this excess of riot, and sinking in this superfluity of naughtiness, let us in agony of spirit plead with God at once on their behalf. Oh, for an immediate entrance of the light into their souls! Lord, open their eyes, that they may see! Lord, cause them to start back from the beginnings of sin, which are as the breaking out of the water-floods! O Saviour, quench in them the spark of evil ere it grows into a fire, and rages to a conflagration!

III. I must now close by mentioning what OUR HOPE is about men when we pray this prayer for them, as I have been doing all along—"Lord, open the young man's eyes, that he may see!" What is our hope in reference to this? What will they see if the heavenly eye-salve be applied?

Elisha, no doubt, felt that the answer to his prayer would be precisely what it really was. "The Lord opened the eyes of the young man; and he saw: and, behold, the mountain was full of horses and chariots of fire round about Elisha." We want men's eyes to be opened, *that they may know, first, that spiritual forces really exist.* The things which we see are not the only real things, nor even the most real things. The things that are seen are temporal; they are, in truth, but shadows of the unseen. The substantial realities are not seen by these poor eyes: the substance is only perceived by our true selves. All that is visible is the mere shadow: the very image of the things is out of sight. Faith teaches us to believe in the existence of that most glorious of all spirits, the great God, in whom we live, and move, and have our being. Faith reveals to the heart the existence of that divine and ever-adorable Person, the Lord Jesus Christ, who is at this hour with his church, and will abide with her to the end of the world. Faith also makes us know the existence, and power, and presence of the Holy Ghost, who dwelleth with believers, and is in them, working out the eternal purpose of God in their sanctification. No knowledge is more sublime than to know the Trinity in Unity; Father, Son, and Holy Ghost, one Jehovah. When we come to realize that the Lord God is the source of all things; that God hath made us, and not we ourselves, and that all things come into being by his sovereign will and power; then we come to recognize his presence, to consult his will, and to lean upon his might. God becomes real in our thought and apprehension. Since he whom we cannot see nevertheless supporteth all things that are, we feel that the invisible is the basis of all things. Oh, that we could get men's minds out of these time-worn ruts of things seen, these narrow bounds of space, and time, and seeing, and handling! Oh, that they could rise into the region where the dim faculties, which are bounded by so small a circle, would give place to perceptions which know the infinite, the eternal, the true, the divine! Oh, that the human mind, which was made in the image of God, could find itself at home with God, whose child it may become, by a second birth, of the living and incorruptible seed, by the Word of God, which liveth and abideth for ever!

Verily, if we get our eyes open, *we shall begin to recognize that God is greater than this world,* and all worlds; and then the mighty truths, which concern his way of mercy in Christ Jesus, will ennoble the soul. Then shall we become true comrades of those bright messengers of God that fly to and fro, fulfilling the behests of the Most High. That there are devils, I think no Christian man will ever doubt; for at certain seasons we have been sadly conscious of a singularly terrible presence, with which our souls have been in agonizing conflict. In that fearful battle it has gone hard with us; our armour has been battered, our comfort has been grievously wounded, and our courage badly mauled. We have been saved as by the skin of our teeth. We hardly knew how to hold on at all, we were so sore beset by unnatural temptations, and suggestions nothing less than infernal. Then, at the Lord's rebuke, this great adversary has taken sudden flight, and angels have come, and ministered to us new joys, and fruits of consolation, fresh from the tree of life. Then have we enjoyed communion with unseen messengers of God, who have seemed to bind up our wounds, and bring us on our way, and whisper peace. Did not an angel come to strengthen our Lord in Gethsemane? Have we not, in our measure, enjoyed a similar visitation? It is a grand thing to see the hosts of God attending us, and to know that bright convoys of these shining ones will come to salute us at the last. It is a great gain to have the eyes opened, to see the Lord's goodness and mercy following us all the days of our life, and ourselves, even here, dwelling in the house of the Lord for evermore. Open your eyes to spiritual things, and at once you are encouraged. The present is grievous, while you know only the visible; but the wilderness blossoms as the rose when you see the invisible. Project yourself beyond this narrow region, and behold the infinite, and sources of joy spring up around you everywhere. Poverty is forgotten in the midst of such riches; and even pain and disease have lost their sting.

Elisha's young attendant, when his eyes were opened, saw, next, that *God's people are safe.* He perceived that there were more with Elisha, after all, than could possibly be against him, and he felt that he himself was safe as the servant of the servant of God. Thus he believed in his master's God, and found a shelter from his own fears. The invaders were flesh and blood, but the defenders were of fire, and thus were able to consume the adversaries at once. He saw, and saw it so joyfully, that God's horses of fire, and chariots of fire, were more than a match for all the forces of evil. I pray that the eyes of every Christian person here may be so opened that they shall never doubt that the powers on the side of truth and righteousness and God are, after all, mightier than the hosts of evil. It may be that you live among those who scoff at your faith, and despise all that you hold dear; indeed, it seems that, wherever you turn, everybody is against you in this day of doubt. I think I hear you cry, with David, "My soul is among lions: and I lie even among them that are set on fire, even the sons of men, whose teeth are spears and arrows, and their tongue a sharp sword." Courage, my comrade, God is near thee! His angels are keeping watch and ward about thee! We are not alone, for the Father is with us. Oh, that our eyes may be so opened as to see that more are they that are with us than all that are against us! Indeed, "if God be for us, who can be against us?" Let us be strangers to fear. In holy confidence, let us be "stedfast, unmoveable, always abounding in the work of the Lord." Never allow a doubt as to the ultimate issue. Is God himself your shield, and your exceeding great reward? Then, what can man do unto you? Perhaps, within a month, some of you, to whom I now speak, may be in so severe a fight that you will be almost driven to throw down your weapons in utter despair, saying, "How can I stand against so many? —I that am so feeble?" I beseech you, remember this warning. Have not I told you of it? I would plead with you to play the man. Gird up the loins of your mind; be sober, and hope to the end; for if the Lord has opened your eyes, you will perceive that you are on the winning side, and that HE is coming soon who will smite his enemies upon the cheekbone. If you are on the side of God, and of his truth; if you do the right; if you believe in the Lord Jesus; if you commit yourself to the keeping of the hand which was pierced with the nails; heaven and earth may pass away, but the Lord can never desert you. The skies may be rolled up like a shrivelled parchment scroll, and all the things that are seen may melt away; like baseless fabrics of a vision, earth and sea may vanish; but a believing soul must live, and triumph, and be exalted to a throne with Christ; for he hath said, "Because I live, ye shall live also." Hold fast your integrity. Believe the truth of God even to the end; for the Lord Jesus will not fail, nor be discouraged, till all his foes are beneath his feet.

If your eyes are opened, you will know that *saints are honoured by their Lord.* See! he despatches his squadrons to be a body-guard to one of them; would not you wish for such honours? See here the secret of the peace which abides with the man of God: as he has meat to eat that men know not of, so has he company that men cannot see. He lives like a prince in the centre of a camp, and sleeps securely. Faith makes the difference between the tranquil prophet and his frightened boy. Oh, that you would believe in the Lord Jesus Christ, and so enter into his peace! May this be the red-letter day in which your eyes shall be opened to see spiritual things, and you shall begin to live a spiritual life! For this I have prayed. For this let us all breathe for a moment a silent prayer. (Here followed an interval of silence, and then the preacher spoke in prayer.) "Lord, I pray thee, open the young man's eyes, that he may see: yea, Lord, open the eyes of all the blind among us, for Jesus' sake! Amen."

12 An Appeal to Children of Godly Parents

"My son, keep thy father's commandment, and forsake not the law of thy mother: bind them continually upon thine heart, and tie them about thy neck. When thou goest, it shall lead thee; when thou sleepest, it shall keep thee; and when thou awakest, it shall talk with thee. For the commandment is a lamp; and the law is light; and reproofs of instruction are the way of life."—Proverbs vi. 20—23.

You have here before you the advice of King Solomon, rightly reckoned to be one of the wisest of men; and verily he must be wise indeed who could excel in wisdom the son of David, the King of Israel. It is worth while to listen to what Solomon has to say; it must be good for the most intelligent young person to listen, and to listen carefully, to what so experienced a man as Solomon has to say to young men. But I must remind you that a greater than Solomon is here, for the Spirit of God inspired the Proverbs. They are not merely jewels from earthly mines, but they are also precious treasures from the heavenly hills; so that the advice we have here is not only the counsel of a wise man, but the advice of that Incarnate Wisdom who speaks to us out of the Word of God. Would you become the sons of wisdom? Come and sit at the feet of Solomon. Would you become spiritually wise? Come and hear what the Spirit of God has to say by the mouth of the wise man.

In considering this subject, I am going, first of all, to show you that *true godliness*, of which the wise man here speaks, *comes to many of us recommended by parental example*: "My son, keep thy father's commandment, and forsake not the law of thy mother: bind them continually upon thine heart, and tie them about thy neck." But, in addition to that, *true religion comes to us commended by practical uses*, by its beneficial effect upon our lives: "When thou goest, it shall lead thee; when thou sleepest, it shall keep thee; and when thou awakest.

it shall talk with thee. For the commandment is a lamp; and the law is light; and reproofs of instruction are the way of life."

I. Now, in the first place, I want to show you that TRUE RELIGION COMES TO MANY OF US RECOMMENDED BY PARENTAL EXAMPLE.

Unhappily, it is not so with all of you. There are some who had an evil example in their childhood, and who never learnt anything that was good from their parents. I adore the sovereignty of divine grace that there are among us to-night many who are the first in their families that ever made a profession of faith in Christ. They were born and brought up in the midst of everything that was opposed to godliness; yet here they are, they can themselves hardly tell you how, brought out from the world as Abraham was brought from Ur of the Chaldees. The Lord in his grace has taken one of a city, and two of a family, and brought them to Zion. You, dear friends, have special cause for thankfulness; but it should be a note to be entered in your diary, that your children shall not be subjected to the same disadvantages as you yourselves suffered. Since the Lord has looked in love upon you, let your households be holiness to the Lord, and so bring up your children that they shall have every advantage that religious training can give, and every opportunity to serve the living God.

But there are many among us, I believe the larger proportion of those gathered here, who have had the immense privilege of godly training. Now, to my mind, it seems that *a father's experience is the best evidence* that a young man can have of the truth of anything. My father would not say that which was false anywhere to anyone; but I am sure that he would not say it to his son; and if, after serving God for fifty years, he has found religion to be a failure, even if he had not the courage to communicate it to the whole world, I feel persuaded that he would have whispered in my ear, "My son, I have misled you. I was mistaken, and I have found it out." But when I saw the old man, the other day, he had no such information to convey to me. Our conversation was concerning the faithfulness of God; and he delights to tell of the faithfulness of God to him and to his father, my dear grandfather, who has now gone up above. How often have they told me that, in a long lifetime of testing and proving the promises, they have found them all true, and they could say, in the language of the hymn,—

> " 'Tis religion that can give
> Sweetest pleasures while we live ;
> 'Tis religion must supply
> Solid comfort when we die."

As for myself, if I had found out that I was mistaken, I should not have been so foolish as to rejoice that my sons should follow the same way of life, and should addict themselves with all their might to preaching the same truth that I delight to proclaim. Dear son, if thou hast a godly father, believe that the religion upon which he has fixed his faith is true. He tells thee that it is so; he is, at any rate, a sincere and honest witness to thee, I beseech thee, therefore, forsake not thy father's God.

Then I think that one of the most tender bonds that can ever bind man or woman is the affection of a mother. Many would, perhaps, break away from the law of the father; but the love of the mother, who among us can break away from that? So, next, *a mother's affection is the best of arguments.* You remember how she prayed for you. Among your earliest recollections is that of her taking you between her knees, and teaching you to say,—

> "Gentle Jesus, meek and mild,
> Look upon a little child."

Perhaps you have tried to disbelieve, but your mother's firm faith prevents it. I have heard of one who said that he could easily have been an infidel if it had not been for his mother's life and his mother's death. Yes, these are hard arguments to get over; and I trust that you will not get over them. You remember well her quiet patience in the house when there was much that might have ruffled her. You remember her gentleness with you when you were going a little wild. You hardly know, perhaps, how you cut her to the heart, how her nights were sleepless because her boy did not love his mother's God. I do charge you, by the love you bear her, if you have received any impressions that are good, cherish them, and cast them not aside. Or if you have received no such impressions, yet at least let the sincerity of your mother, for whom it was impossible to have been untrue, —let the deep affection of your mother, who could not, and would not, betray you into a lie,—persuade you that there is truth in this religion which now, perhaps, some of your companions are trying to teach you to deride. "My son, keep thy father's commandment, and forsake not the law of thy mother."

I think that, to any young man, or any young woman either, who has had a godly father and mother, the best way of life that they can mark out for themselves is to *follow the road in which their father's and mother's principles would conduct them.* Of course, we make great advances on the old folks, do we not? The young men are wonderfully bright and intelligent, and the old people are a good deal behind them. Yes, yes; that is the way we talk before our beards have grown. Possibly, when we have more sense, we shall not be quite so conceited of it. At any rate, I, who am not very old, and who dare not any longer call myself young, venture to say that, for myself, I desire nothing so much as to continue the traditions of my household. I wish to find no course but that which shall run parallel with that of those who have gone before me. And I think, dear friends, that you who have seen the holy and happy lives of Christian ancestors will be wise to pause a good deal before you begin to make a deviation, either to the right or to the left, from the course of those godly ones. I do not believe that he begins life in a way which God is likely to bless, and which he himself will, in the long run, judge to be wise, who begins with the notion that he shall upset everything, that all that belonged to his godly family shall be cast to the winds. I do not seek to have heirlooms of gold or silver; but, though I die a thousand deaths, I can never give up my father's God, my grandsire's God, and *his* father's God, and *his* father's God. I must hold this to be the chief possession that I have; and I pray young men and women to think the same. Do not stain the glorious traditions of noble lives that have been handed down to you; do not disgrace your father's shield, bespatter not the escutcheons of your honoured predecessors by any sins and transgressions on your part. God help you to feel that the best way of leading a noble life will be to do as they did who trained you in God's fear!

Solomon tells us to do two things with the teachings which we have learned of our parents. First he says, "Bind them continually upon thine heart," for *they are worthy of loving adherence.* Show that you love these things by binding them upon your heart. The heart is the vital point; let godliness lie there, love the things of God. If we could take young men and women, and make them professedly religious without their truly loving godliness, that would be simply to make them hypocrites, which is not what we desire. We do not want you to say that you believe what you do not believe, or that you rejoice in what you do not rejoice in. But our prayer—and, oh, that it might be your prayer, too!—is that you may be helped to bind these things about your heart. They are worth living for, they are worth dying for, they are worth more than all the world besides, the immortal principles of the divine life which comes from the death of Christ. "Bind them continually upon thine heart."

And then Solomon, because he would not have us keep these things secret as if we were ashamed of them, adds, "and tie them about thy neck," for *they are worthy of boldest display.* Did you ever see my Lord Mayor wearing his chain of office? He is not at all ashamed to wear it. And the sheriffs with their brooches; I have a lively recollection of the enormous size to which those ornaments attain; and they take care to wear them, too. Now then, you who have any love to God, tie your religion about your neck. Do not be ashamed of it, put it on as an ornament, wear it as the mayor does his chain. When you go into company, never be ashamed to say that you are a Christian; and if there is any company where you cannot go as a Christian, well, do not go there at all. Say to yourself, "I will not be where I could not introduce my Master; I will not go where he could not go with me." You will find that resolve to be a great help to you in the choice of where you will go, and where you will not go; therefore bind it upon your heart, tie it about your neck. God help you to do this, and so to follow those godly ones who have gone before you!

I hope that I am not weak in wishing that some here may be touched by affection to their parents. I have had very sorrowful sights, sometimes, in the course of my ministry. A dear father, an honest, upright, godly man, is perhaps present; but he will not mind my saying what lines of grief I saw upon his face when he came to say to me, "Oh, sir, my boy is in prison!" I am sure that, if his boy could have seen his father's face as I saw it, it would have been worse than prison to him. I have known young men who have come to this Tabernacle with their parents,—nice boys, too, they were,—and they have gone into situations in the city, where they have been tempted to steal, and they have yielded to the tempter, and they have lost their character. Sometimes, the deficiency has been met, and they have been rescued from a criminal's career; but, alas, sometimes they have fallen into the hands of a wicked woman, and then woe betide them! Occasionally, it has seemed to be sheer wantonness and wickedness that has made them act unrighteously. I wish I could fetch those young men—I do not suppose that they are here to-night—and let them see, not merely the misery they will bring upon themselves, but show them their mother at home when news came that John had lost his position because he had been acting dishonestly, or give them a glimpse of the father's face when the evil tidings reached him. The poor man stood aghast; he said, "There was never a stain upon the character of any of my family before." If the earth had opened under the godly man's feet, or if the good mother could have gone down straight into the grave, they would have preferred it to the lifelong tribulation which has come upon them. Therefore, I charge you, young man, or young woman, do not kill the parents who gave you life, do not disgrace those who brought you up; but I pray you, instead thereof, seek the God of your father, and the God of your mother, and give yourselves to the Lord Jesus Christ, and live wholly to him.

II. Now I must turn to my second point, which is, that TRUE RELIGION COMES TO US COMMENDED BY PRACTICAL USES. This is a less sentimental argument than the one I have been pleading; but, to many, vital godliness appeals because of its immense utility in the actual everyday life of men.

Solomon tells us, first, that *true godliness serves us for instruction:* "For the commandment is a lamp." If thou wouldst know all that thou oughtest to know, read this Book. If thou wouldst know in thy heart that which shall be for thy present and eternal good, love this Book, believe the truth it teaches, and obey it, "for the commandment is a lamp."

Next, *true religion serves us for direction:* "and the law is light." If we want to know what we should do, we cannot do better than yield ourselves up to the guidance of the Divine Spirit, and take this Word as our map, for—

> "'Tis like the sun, a heavenly light,
> That guides us all the day;
> And through the dangers of the night,
> A lamp to lead our way."

Solomon also tells us that *true religion guides us under all circumstances.* He says, in the 22nd verse, that when we are active, there is nothing like true godliness to help us: "When thou goest, it shall lead thee." He tells us that, when we are resting, there is nothing better than this for our preservation: "When thou sleepest, it shall keep thee." And when we are just waking, there is nothing better than this with which to delight the mind: "When thou awakest, it shall talk with thee." I do not intend to expand those three thoughts except just to say this. When thou art busiest, thy religion shall be thy best help. When thy hands are full of toil, and thy head is full of thought, nothing can do thee more service than to have a God to go to, a Saviour to trust in, a heaven to look forward to. And when thou goest to thy bed to sleep, or to be sick, thou canst have nothing better to smooth thy pillow, and to give thee rest, than to know that thou art forgiven through the precious blood of Christ, and saved in the Lord with an everlasting salvation. Often, ere I fall asleep, I say to myself those words of Watts,—

> "Sprinkled afresh with pardoning blood,
>   I lay me down to rest,
> As in the embraces of my God,
>   Or on my Saviour's breast;"

and there is no more delicious sleep in the world than that sleep which, even in dreams, keeps near to Christ. Some of us know what it is, even in those wanderings of our mind in sleep, not to quit the holy ground of communion with our Lord. It is not always so, but it is sometimes so; and even then, when the mind has lost power to control its thoughts, even the thoughts seem to dance, like Miriam, to the praise of God. Oh, happy men, whose religion is their protection even in their sleep! And then Solomon says, "when thou awakest, it shall talk with thee." This Bible is a wonderful talking-book; there is a great mass of blessed talk in this precious volume. It has told me a great many of my faults; it would tell you yours if you would let it. It has told me much to comfort me; and it has much to tell you if you will but incline your ear to it. It is a book that is wonderfully communicative; it knows all about you, all the ins and outs of where you are, and where you ought to be, it can tell you everything. The best communion that a man can have is when he commences with God in prayer and the reading of the Word: "When thou awakest, it shall talk with thee."

I have hurried over that point because I want to say something else to you. Dear friends, those of you who are unconverted, our great anxiety is that you should know the Lord at once; and our reason is this, that *it will prepare you for the world to come.* Whatever that world may be, full of vast mysteries, yet no man is so prepared to launch upon the unknown sea as the one who is reconciled to God, who believes in the Lord Jesus Christ, who trusts him, and rejoices in the pardon of his sin through the great atoning sacrifice, and experiences in his own heart the marvellous change which has made him a new creature in Christ Jesus. The great reason, I say again, why we wish to have our dear friends converted, is that they may be ready for the world to come. You will soon die, all of you: I think it was last Sunday evening that there sat, in that pew just over there, a friend who was generally here in the morning and evening; but on Wednesday he died quite suddenly. He appeared to be in good health, but he died at the railway station, away from home. That seat where he used to sit ought to have a warning voice to all of us, crying aloud, "Prepare to meet thy God." It might have been myself; it might have been any of these friends around me on the platform; it might have been any of you in the congregation. Who can tell who will go this week? Probably some one or other of us (our number is so large) will be taken away ere another Sabbath bell shall be heard.

I think that is a very good reason for seeking the Lord, that you may be prepared for eternity. One day this week, I saw an aged friend, who cannot live much longer; she is eighty-six, and her faculties are failing her; but she said to me, "I have no fear, I have no fear of death; I am on the Rock, I am on the Rock Christ Jesus. I know whom I have believed, and I know where I am going." It was delightful to hear the aged saint speak like that; and we are always hearing such talk from our dear friends when they are going home, they never seem to have any doubts. I have known some who, while they were well, had many doubts; but when they came to die, they seemed to have none at all, but were joyously confident in Christ.

But there is another reason why we want our friends converted, and that is, *that they may be prepared for this life.* I do not know what kind of life you have set before yourself. Perhaps I may be addressing some young men who are going to the University, and they hope to have lives consecrated to learning, and crowned with honour. Possibly, some here have no prospect but that of working hard to earn their bread with the sweat of their brow; some have begun to lay bricks, or to drive the plane, or to wield the pen. There are all sorts of ways of mortal life; but there is no better provision and preparation for any kind of life on earth than to know the Lord, and to have a new heart and a right spirit. He that rules millions of men will do it better with the grace of God in his heart; and he that had to be a slave would be the happier in his lot for having the grace of God in his heart. You that are old and you that are young, you that are masters and you that are servants, true religion cannot disqualify you for playing your part here in the great drama of life; but the best preparation for that part, if it is a part that ought to be played, is to know the Lord, and feel the power of divine grace upon your soul.

Let me just show you how this is the case. The man who lives before God, who calls God his Father, and feels the Spirit of God working within him a hatred of sin and a love of righteousness, he is the man who will be *conscientious in the discharge of his duties;* and, you know, that is the kind of man, and the kind of woman, too, that we want nowadays. We have so many people who want looking after; if you give them anything to do, they will do it quickly enough if you stand and look on; but the moment you turn your back, they will do it as slovenly, or as slowly, and as badly as can be. They are eye-servants only. If you were to advertise for an eye-servant, I do not suppose anybody would come to you; yet they might come in shoals, for there are plenty of them about. Well now, a truly Christian man, a man who is really converted, sees that he serves God in doing his duty to his fellow-men. "Thou God seest me," is the power that ever influences him; and he desires to be conscientious in the discharge of his duties whatever those duties may be. I once told you the story of the servant girl who said that she hoped she was converted. Her minister asked her this question, "What evidence can you give of your conversion?" She gave this among a great many other proofs, but it was not a bad one; she said, "Now, sir, I always sweep *under* the mats." It was a small matter, but if you carry out in daily life that principle of sweeping under the mats, that is the kind of thing we want. Many people have a little corner where they stow away all the fluff and the dust, and the room looks as if it was nicely swept, but it is not. There is a way of doing everything so that nothing is really done, but that is not the case where there is grace in the heart. Grace in the heart makes a man feel that he would wish to live wholly to God, and serve God in serving man. If you get that grace, you will have a grand preparation for life as well as for death.

The next thing is, that a man who has a new heart has imparted to him *a purity which preserves him in the midst of temptation.* Oh, this dreadful city of London! I wonder that God endures the filth of it. I frequently converse with good young men, who come up from the country to their first situation in London, and the first week they live in London is a revelation to them which makes their hair almost stand on end. They see what they never dreamt of. Well now, you young fellows who have just come to London, perhaps this is your first Sunday, give yourselves to the Lord at once, I pray you. Yield yourselves to Jesus Christ to-night, for another week in London may be your damnation. Only a week in London may have led you into acts of impurity that shall ruin you for ever. Before you have gone into those things, devote yourselves to God, and to his Christ, that with pure hearts and with right spirits you may be preserved from "the pestilence that walketh in darkness, and the destruction that wasteth at noonday," in this terribly wicked city. There is no hope for you young men and young women in this great world of wickedness unless your hearts are right towards God. If you go in thoroughly to follow the Lamb whithersoever he goeth, he will keep and preserve you even to the end; but if you do not give yourselves to the Lord, whatever good resolutions you may have formed, you are doomed—I am sure you are—to be carried away with the torrents of iniquity that run down our streets to-day. Purity of heart, then, which comes from faith in Christ, is a splendid preparation for life.

So also is *truthfulness of speech.* Oh, what a wretched thing it is when people will tell lies! Now, the heart that is purified by the grace of God, hates the thought of a lie. The man speaks the truth, the whole truth, and nothing but the truth; and he is the man who shall pass through life unscathed, and shall be honoured, and in the long run successful. He may have to suffer for a time through his truthfulness; but, in the end, nothing shall clear a way for him so well as being true in thought and word and deed.

If you love the Lord with all your heart, you will also learn *honesty in dealing;* and that is a grand help in life. I know that the trickster does sometimes seem to succeed for a time; but what is his success? It is a success which is only another name for ruin. Oh, dear sirs, if all men could be made honest, how much more of happiness there would be in the world! And the way to be upright among men is to be sincere towards God, and to have the Spirit of God dwelling within you.

Again, true religion is of this value, that *it comforts a man under great troubles.* You do not expect many troubles, my young friend, but you will have them. You expect that you will be married, and then your troubles will be over; some say that *then* they begin. I do not endorse that statement; but I am sure that they are not over, for there is another set of trials that begin then. But you are going to get out of your apprenticeship, and then it will be all right; will it? Journeymen do not always find it so. But you do not mean always to be a journeyman; you are going to be a little master. Ask the masters whether everything is pleasant with them in these times. If you want to escape trouble altogether, you had better go up in a balloon; and then I am sure that you would be in trouble for fear of going up too high or coming down too fast. But troubles will come; and what is there that can preserve a man in the midst of trouble like feeling that things are safe in his Father's hands? If you can say, "I am his child, and all things are working together for my good. I have committed myself entirely into the hands of him who cannot err, and will never do me an unkindness," why, sir, you have on a breastplate which the darts of care cannot pierce, you are shod with the preparation of the gospel of peace, and you may tread on the briars of the wilderness with an unwounded foot.

True religion will also build up in you *firmness of character*, and that is another quality that I want to see in our young people nowadays. We have some splendid men in this place, and some splendid women, too. I should not be afraid, if the devil himself were to preach here, that he would pervert them from the faith; and if all the new heresies that can rise were to be proclaimed in their presence, they know too well what the truth is ever to be led astray. But, on the other hand, we have a number of people who are led by their ears. If I pull their ear one way, they come after me; if they happen to go somewhere else, and somebody pulls their ear the other way, they go after him. There are lots of people who never do their own thinking, but put it out, as they put out their washing; they do not think of doing it at home. Well now, these people are just like the chaff on the threshing-floor, and when the wind begins to blow, away they go. Do not be like that. Dear young sons and daughters of the church-members here, know the Lord. May he reveal himself to you at once; and when you do know him, and get a grip of the gospel, bind it to your heart, and tie it about your neck, and say, "Yes, I am going to follow in the footsteps of those I love, and especially in the footsteps of the Lord Jesus Christ.

> " ' Through floods and flames, if Jesus lead,
>   I'll follow where he goes.' "

God help you to do it! But first believe in the Lord Jesus Christ; trust yourselves wholly to him, and he will give you grace to stand fast even to the end.